Thierry Leprévost & Georges Bernage

HASTINGS 1066

Norman Cavalry and Saxon Infantry

With a contribution by Eric Groult

HEIMDAL

1066 - Hastings and Bayeux

The Battle of Hastings which was fought on 14 October 1066, was a major event, and 11th century Normandy had become one of the most powerful territories in western Europe. Thanks to its strong base of Scandinavian immigrants the territory benefited from a dense and well settled population as well as a strong central power with a numerous aristocracy loyal to the Duke of Normandy. The Norman state combined Scandinavian pragmatism with its Frankish institutions which had their origins in the Gallo-Roman epoch. Orderliness, organisation and a dynamic spirit were the factors which favoured Norman expansion. One should not forget that at that period that the numerous landless sons of the many small noble families of western Normandy set off to conquer southern Italy and Sicily, creating a state there which balanced effectiveness with tolerance, highly regarded by Italian historians.

The power of Normandy was well served by a military system well in advance of its time, which had proved itself in Italy and was to do so again in England where it was to have a profound effect on the institutions, the architecture and even the language – modern English still has many Norman influences. That great island which was never again to be invaded, emerged strengthened and empowered from the Norman conquest. The English knights who disembarked in France three centuries later were far better able to fight at what was the start of the Hundred Years War – Hastings in reverse!

This book makes considerable use of extracts from the Bayeux Tapestry as without that remarkable embroidery over 70 metres long, the Battle of Hastings would have remained an important event but one which would be difficult to imagine. The Tapestry has supplied us with an enormous amount of information about 11th century civilisation : clothing, weapons, harness, ships, shipbuilding, hair styles, tools and farming implements, etc. Thanks to the Bayeux Tapestry we can enter into the spirit of the 11th century with our eyes open rather then having to rely on a few archaeological finds and thanks also to the hundreds of enthusiasts who are devoted to period re-enactment. Their researches have allowed us a far better appreciation of the clothing and equipment of the period. There were more than three and a half thousand of them at Hastings in October 2000 taking part in a painstaking re-enactment of the battle on the actual sites, sponsored by English Heritage and several British re-enactment groups. These 3,500 participants had taken enormous pains to recreate their equipment of the period. Thierry Leprevost was there representing Normandy Television, and Erik Groult took part in the battle in order to gain a better understanding of the event. The writer of these lines was also in the thick of things, camera in hand but disguised under the robe and hat of an 11th century man, to help you to relive this event.

This book is above all, instructional – it describes a historical event, illustrated with the Bayeux Tapestry and pictures of the re-enactment, aiming to get to the heart of the story. It also allows us as faithfully as possible to recreate the equipment of that epoch and to chart the course of the battle. This book is a contribution towards a better understanding of one of the great periods of history – the 11th century.

Georges Bernage

- This book was conceived by Georges Bernage.

- The text of the historic chapters is by Thierry Leprevost. Georges Bernage designed and wrote the chapter, "The fighting man of 1066", as well as selecting the illustrations and writing the captions. The English text version in by Anthony Kemp.

- Illustrations : The extracts from the Bayeux Tapestry were provided by the City of Bayeux which was also involved in the creation of this book. The Blois Museum kindly provided some illustrations of archaeological artefacts. The photographs taken during the re-enactment of the battle in October 2000 are by Georges Bernage (G.B. or unattributed), Thierry Leprevost (T.L.) or by Sébastien Belétoile (S.B.)

- Graphic design by Eric Groult who is also responsible for the battlefield planc.

- Typesetting and page layout : Marie-Claire Passerieu and Christel Lebret.

Editions Heimdal - Château de Damigny - BP 61350 - 14406 BAYEUX Cedex - Tél. : 02.31.51.68.68 - Fax : 02.31.51.68.60 -
E-mail : Editions.Heimdal@wanadoo.fr

ISBN 2 84048 150 2

A forest on the sea

William Duke of Normandy was alone. In the east, the first glimmer of dawn which stretched from horizon to horizon revealed the admiral's ship the *Mora*, given to him by the Duchess Matilda. Where was the rest of his fleet? Where were the thousand ships carrying his invasion army? All around him the sea was empty.

They has sailed the evening before from St. Valéry at the end of a day on which his spies had informed him that the King of Norway, Harold Hardrada, had finally arrived in the Tyne eight days earlier, and he had been waiting a long time for the opening of this northern front. Ever since the spring of that year 1066 the two men had had an agreement : while the Viking created a diversion in northern England, the Duke of Normandy would effect a landing in the south. Thus the kingdom would be caught between the jaws of a pincer and thus be at his mercy They would divide the spoils in the same way : the north for Norway and the south for Normandy, at least for starters.

In reality William had been expecting this movement since the summer, while under his eyes the fleet for the conquest was being built in the lagoon at Varraville facing the town of Dives, where God, at the beginning of the century, had caused a miraculous carved wooden statue of Christ to be washed up.

His aim was to cross the Channel in a straight line towards the end of July or the beginning of August, aiming for the Isle of Wight, quite near to Winchester, the capital of Wessex, which he counted on being able to capture. But the southerly wind did not abate and anyway, the diversion he needed did not take place. On top of all that, Tostig, the estranged brother of the Harold, King of England, had undertaken unsuccessful harassing operations against his sovereign. According to intelligence reaching

William, Tostig had taken refuge with his friend, Malcolm, King of Scotland, where he himself was awaiting the arrival of Harold of Norway on the English coast, before making a reappearance. At the same time, William heard that Harold of England's fleet, 700 ships strong and charged with the protection of the south coast, had been disarmed and put into storage on 8 September, because the King did not believe in any Norman offensive before the following spring. Thus the men of the fyrd, the English citizen levies recruited from the peasantry and the townsfolk whose lives were not solely devoted to arms, had been sent home.

Thus everything seemed to be coming together for Duke William who had changed his plans and embarked shortly before dawn on 12 September 1066 the immense camp which covered more than 20 square kilometres to the west and south west of Dives, housing more than 7,000 warriors ready to try conclusions with the English, as well as at least 1,000 servants. At a cost of the sinking of several ships which were shattered against the cliffs of the Pays de Caux, they had cruised east-

wards as far as Vimeu, a fief belonging to the Duchy of Normandy which was held by Guy of Ponthieu, a vassal of William. There, they had anchored at St. Valéry in the Somme estuary where they waited for more favourable winds.

There was no longer any question of steering for the Isle of Wight : their new destination was to be Pevensey Bay, not far from Hastings and to the south of London. On 28 September, when the wind appeared to be favourable, William was thinking of the Winds of History which he had never previously yielded

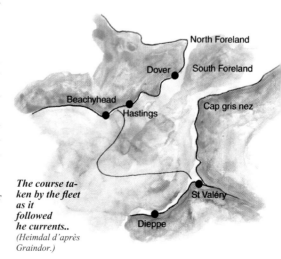

The course taken by the fleet as it followed he currents..
(Heimdal d'après Graindor.)

(T.L.)

to. There was another reason, less convincing, which had persuaded William to spread the story of a contrary wind for changing the crossing. He let Harold Hardrada know that his fleet had been pinned down for months on the southern shore of the Channel on account of unfavourable winds and persuaded

him to move alone against Harold of England before the arrival of the Norwegian winter. Thus, whatever the result of their confrontation, William would have his hands free for a successful landing.

William had thought of everything. He set sail at the end of the afternoon, carried westwards

by the current towards Ushant where the fleet changed course to the north, straight for Pevensey. Towards midnight, just as the first quarter of the moon dipped below the horizon a cloud of will o'the wisps danced over the waves, guided by the highest of the lanterns, that of the *Mora*, just underneath the

(T.L.)

TRAN · SIVIT · ETVENIT · AD

copper weather vane which capped the mast of that fine ship.

Then the sails were furled and the hove to for a few hours rest as William did not want to risk a night landing, preferring to wait. Before dawn as the signals were given by trumpets and flags, the small ships once again got underway , their sails full of wind in the darkness of the night, steering by the North Star at the base of the tail of the constellation of the Little Bear.

William though that he had everything worked out, but as dawn broke on 29 September, the day dedicated to Michael, the patron saint of the Normans, his ships had disappeared!

The *Mora* was alone, facing the distant shoreline of England which was emerging gradually through the morning mist, so near but all at once so far — William's inheritance. He was frightened. Had God abandoned him?

It was perhaps as well that it was the Pope who was supporting him in this venture. The Papal banner which Alexander II had sent William strengthened his faith and accompanied him on his warlike mission. At the same time he wore round his neck a precious relic set in gold — a tooth of the first Pope, Saint Peter.

To cement his agreement with Harold, Duke William promised him one of his daughters, Aelfgyfa (Adelise in French). In this scene from the Bayeux Tapestry, the embroiderer has written her name in the Anglo-Saxon way which furnishes further proof that it was made in England.

This was also why William was setting out to fight an oathbreaker. Harold, Earl of Wessex and son of Godwin, who two years earlier had sworn on the holiest relics of Bayeux Cathedral to respect the wishes of Edward the Confessor, King of England who had clearly stated that his cousin William should inherit the throne. In order to seal their agreement, William had offered one of his daughters, Adelise, in mar-

riage to Harold, but the previous spring, the latter had married Aldgyth, the widow of the Welsh King, Gruffyd ap Llywelyn. There was, however, worse to come.

On 5 January 1066, Edward the Confessor died and the following day, Harold Godwinson assumed the throne of the dead king, in contravention of his promise given two years before and thus placing himself at odds with the whole of Christian Europe who regarded him as a usurper and oathbreaker. William was afraid because if he lost his fleet, he would also lose Normandy. With him had embarked the finest of his men, his two brothers, Robert and Odo, as well as all the great noblemen of the Duchy- In addition there were other lords who had come from elsewhere, plus volunteers from Brittany, Frenchmen, Flemings, men from Picardy, Angevins, and Poitevins plus many mercenaries - archers, crossbowmen and infantry, all keen to enrich themselves by taking part in the adventure.

A powerful prince, devoted to his Norman lands, William alone on the ocean was as nothing. Up on top of the mast the look-out could see nothing but the sky and the sea. 38 years old and after years of successful fighting, everything seemed to have deserted the Duke. Yes, he was

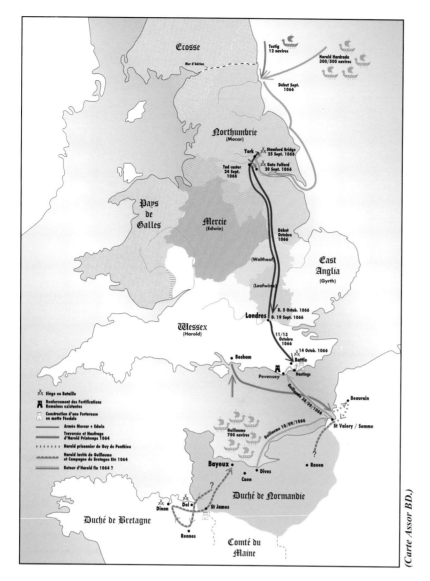

(Carte Assor BD.)

frightened but he could not let his companions see his anguish. All around him mens' throats tightened and there was a fearful silence, but William calmly gave orders to lay the table for a sumptuous meal to be washed down with plentiful hypocras, a scented and spiced wine.

When the meal was over a cry rang out from above them. Clinging to the mast the look-out announced four sails stretched in the wind. Then, the horizon became covered with ships. The look-out shouted that he could see "a forest advancing over the water and each of the trees is carrying a sail".

Immediately a hubbub broke out on board the *Mora*. 3 Holy Virgin, Saint Michael, God has aided us". Better shaped and rigged than the other vessels, and captained by Etienne Airard, the best sailor from Barfleur, the *Mora* had simply outpaced the rest of the fleet. William ordered a red and gold sail to be hoisted which would take him towards his destiny.

(T.L.)

Pevensey

(T.L.)

Once again united, the Ducal fleet saw the land approaching, and the ships were swept in by the rising tide. By a strange coincidence of geography, (the choice, however, was not fortuitous), Pevensey Bay at that time presented many similarities with Dives, the embarkation port where William had fitted out his ships — a broken coastline, a vast lagoon indented with peninsulas and covered with small cultivated islands accessible at low tide, all protected from the sea by a tongue of dunes. During the ensuing centuries, however, both sites have suffered the same fate and become silted up and filled by a patchwork of polders which have caused the original outline of the coast to disappear and the lagoon has been transformed into fields on which seaside resorts have been built.

The effect of surprise was total and there was not a soldier to be seen. Out of that immense fleet, only two ships had missed their destination and came ashore fur-

ther east at Romney in Kent, the inhabitants of which mobilised quickly and massacred the new arrivals. After the battle William avenged them and made the town pay blood money.

Many other ships simply beached on the dunes without damage but the majority slipped through the channel into the lagoon where a fortified enclosure appeared before the eyes of the Normans and their allies. It was the ancient of Anderida, built late in the Roman period as a defence against Saxon invaders, surrounded by stout and well preserved walls constructed in

alternate layers of stone and brick as was customary. Totally abandoned, the partly ruined nut nevertheless high walls enclosed an area of several hectares perched on a rocky outcrop which jutted out into the bay and dominated it. The village of Pevensey was to the west end nestled on the reverse slope — an ideal place for a stopover.

Around nine o'clock in the morning the rivers receded and the flat-bottomed ships dried out. They were mostly identical to the famous long-ships with which William's Viking ances-

tors had ravaged the coasts of the Carolingian Empire from the beginning of the 10th century.

The fleet, however, was not entirely homogenous. In such a short time it had been impossible to build all the vessels to the same design and it had been necessary to call on already existing vessels; built for fishing or freight transport. Some were bought outright, others were hired or requisition and ships from outside Normandy were accepted, supplied by Lords who were taking part in the expedition. How many vessels did the Ducal fleet consist of? The chronicler Wace who came from Jersey, writing at the beginning of the 12th century, stated in his *Roman de Rou* that 696 ships departed from St. Valéry (700 minus four). The figure is far too precise to be ignored. He said that it came from his grandfather who took part in the expedition although we do not know in what capacity. One can assume, however, that he had an important role to play in the logistics. He gave that information to his son, Wace's father.

I do not wish to write down here
Nor undertake to tell
How many nobles, warriors, va-
vasors or knights
The Duke had in his company.
But I do remember, when I was
small
The seven hundred less four
Left from St. Valéry.
Ships, small boats and transport
vessels
Carrying arms and horses.

(Wace Roman de Rou. Verses 6417 to 6428)

Nevertheless, Wace was sure that the 696 corresponded to the more important vessels, those which carried the Lords and the combat troops as well as their horses. Numerous other ships would have embarked the servants, grooms, cooks, carpenters, labourers, and the entire stores : fodder, tenting, spare arms and ammunition and naturally the enormous quantities of wood which would serve to assemble the first Norman fortifications to be built on English soil. Taking all that into account, one can assume a fleet of a thousand ships all told.

The *Mora* was the first to touch the shore because the honour of being the fist to set foot on his inheritance belonged to Duke William, which turned into somewhat of a farce. Under the admiring gaze of hundreds of pairs of eyes, he jumped down onto the beach, took a step, stumbled and fell flat on his face All around him there was consternation and there were cries for help. His companions made the sign of the cross an invoked the Virgin Mary. In a constrained fury the Duke got up slowly, his fingers clenched around sand and pebbles from the beach. Majestically he raised his hand to the sky, and unclenching his fingers, allowed the sand to trickle down in a stream glittering in the morning sunlight.

The Duke was the first to land
And fell on his palms.
On the land echoed the cries
Who all said "a bad omen".
Standing tall the Duke addressed
them
"My Lords! By the splendour of
God!
The land which I have seized in
my hands
Is proof that Heaven has blessed
it.
It is I who truly deserves it."
A man standing there,
Ran towards a cottage and stret-
ching out his hand,
Ripped off a piece of the thatch
And ran back as fast as he could.
"Sire", he said to the Duke, "come
cmose",
This pledge is destined for you.
I have seized it from this land
Because you are in your coun-
try".
The Duke replied, "I accept it,
Because God will cause our
blood to pound".

Rou. Verses 6573 to 6592.

An immense ovation echoed around him. "God be praised. Long Live William. Long Live Normandy".

The vessels which had stranded in the bay clustered together like wasps on a ripe fruit, most of them to the north of the peninsula on which stood the Roman fort where the local fisherman had constructed rudimentary landing stages, the others facing them, on the islands and tongues of land. The bay was covered in ships, and men jumped into the water or pulled up the boats onto the beach, sails were furled and masts dropped in a cacophony of shouts, oaths, swear words, and neighing of horses which echoed all around. The warriors stepped ashore, battered and bruised from a night at sea piled on top of each other, some of whom had been sea sick, jumbled up like beasts among the stores and armaments. Already the archers had formed up into a line ready to repel any attack that might develop.

At the bottom of the cargo spaces for the obvious reasons of stability and safety with only their heads poking out, the horses were impatient to be disembarked. Some were injured, had panicked or had been kicked by their fellows during the constricted voyage but the losses were minimal. The decking above which was built to contain the chargers was dismantled, on which the grooms and sailors sat during the trip. Thanks to wooden struts these large floating stables were stabilised so that threy sloped sideways, emitting a foul stench from the 3,000 cavalry mounts. The horses leapt out one by one according to an efficient method of Arab and Byzantine origin, tried out by the Normans in Sicily in 1061 and 1062, several of whom had joined William's expedition.

Mounted on their chargers, the knights supported the infantry in their task of protecting the encampment while the quartermasters got down to work. The whole area was like a desert island : the inhabitants had not waited for the landing to begin before fleeing from their homes, shocked by the amplitude of the invasion force, in a land where the slightest strange sip always meant pillage, rape and massacre.

The unloading of stores got underway : fighting stores and provisions to feed initially the whole expedition. Wadard, a vassal of William's half brother, Bishop Odo of Bayeux, gave the orders for landing the supplies and his men were charged with combing the locality to round up all the domestic animals they could lay their hands on — sheep, cattle and poultry, down to horses which could be used for carrying supplies.

From the bridge of the *Mora*, .William observed the shore and received reports from his scouts, assuring himself that the delicate operation of disembarkation was running smoothly and taking stock of the crossing. He remembered a cleric who practised astrology who had predicted at St. Valéry that he, William, would have a happy crossing and a victory without a battle. He asked after him, surprised not to see him, and was told that man had drowned.

When the Duke had crossed successfully
And had arrived safe and sound,
He remembered his priest,
Asked for him and looked well.
One of the sailors replied
That the cleric had perished,
And that he had drowned in the sea
When his ship had sunk.
"It does not matter", said the Duke, "its not important.
He did not have much knowledge.
He could divine for me
But not for himself.
If he had been able to see the future,
He would have been able to predict his own death.
Only a fool believes a fortune-teller
Who can foresee something for someone else
But who knows nothing about his own life,
Who says to another person what is then forgotten."

Rou. Verses 6553 to 6570.

By way of the gate that opened to the west of the Roam fort, the troops assembled inside the ancient Anderida which was quickly transformed into a Norman entrenched camp. The aim was to create a shelter for the night, call the roll and collect the force together after the crossing. William, known as the "Bastard" on account of his being born out of wedlock, examined the place and was astonished that the Anglo-Saxons had not garrisoned it for their own defence. Certainly, thanks to his spies, he already knew about the place. The nearby monasteries at Rye and Winchelsea had for a long time been subject to the Abbey of Fécamp, which had enabled him to keep abreast of the military situation on that part of the coast. He, William, would not make the same mis-

The Normans cooked their meals in large cauldrons or over open fires.

take and included the major part of the site into his strategic plan. In the south-east corner of the enclosure he had an inner castle built provided with a high keep to be able to completely control access to the bay, at the exact spot where, at that exact moment and under his orders, his soldiers were pitching their tents for the night.

Powerless, the local Saxons viewed from afar the pillage of their countryside, completely unaware that in the north-eat of England, the tide of history had turned.

By making their landfall in the Tyne estuary the 300 ships of Harold of Norway had joined up with those of Tostig Godwinson, in rebellion against his brother the King of England. Together they pillaged Holdernes and burned Scarborough before sailing up the Tyne on 18 September and then into the Ouse as far as Ricall where they left their boats in the care of a friendly local population, guarded by Prince Olaf,

a son of Harold Hardrada before heading off on foot to York which had a powerful Scandinavian colony at the time.

The brothers Edwin and Morcar, respectively Earls of Mercia and Northumbria awaited them resolutely at the gates of the old city. It was there that the first battle for the Crown of England took place on 20 September.. The Norwegians, joined by the Scots who Tostig had brought with him, English opposed to Harold and mercenaries, notably Flemings, were able to overcome the defenders at considerable cost in casualties and enter the city. Hardrada accepted the surrender, counting on the support of the inhabitants in the battle that was to come.

Harold Godwinson heard this alarming news just when he had demobilised the fyrd, but he hastily assembled what troops he had and left London by the old Roman north road. Riding day

and night in a forced march he reached York on the morning of 25 September. The invasion force had positioned itself about fifteen kilometres away from there at Stamford Bridge where the River Derwent wound slowly through a marshy area. Not expecting the approach of the Anglo Saxons, the Vikings had left their chain mail and breastplates at Ricall with the boats because the early autumn heat had made wearing them unbearable. When they saw the cloud of dust approaching them from the direction of York, their surprise was total and as great as their lack of military preparations. The arms of the troops closing in on them sparkled like rays of sun on a misty glacier They were only two miles away.

Harold Hardrada decided to call his force to arms and sent horsemen towards the boats to summon help, but Ricall was twenty kilometres distant and the Saxons were already on them ! ;

(T.L.)

A group of soldiers was deliberately sacrificed to hold up the advance. A simple wooden bridge over the Derwent separated the belligerents which was so narrow that according to the Nordic sagas, one man in the middle was sufficient to guard it. That Norwegian massacred with his battleaxe anyone who attempted to get across, dispatching 40 Saxons in the process. Finally, a Saxon, climbing into a primitive boast was able to slip under the bridge and stab the hero with a spear, through a gap in the planks of the treadway. Seeing that the situation was desperate, Tostig decided to negotiate with his brother, and Harold offered him Northumbria and a third of his kingdom if he agreed not to fight. As far as Harold of Norway was concerned, however, all he would get was seven feet of good English earth, or perhaps a bit more as he was of above average height. Instead of deciding on an immediate retreat, Hardrada replied that the son of Sigurd had never taken flight in front of his subjects.

The second battle for the mastery of England was a terrible one. After a hail of thrown spears the infantry threw themselves on their opponents in what turned out to be a hand to hand struggle. Caught off balance and overtired, many of the Vikings drowned in the marshes. Harold Hardrada received an arrow in his throat, which was quite a rare feat because there were not many archers in Harold Godwinson's ranks and died just as the expected reinforcements arrived. The latter fought with the energy of despair and caused the Saxons their worst losses of the day, but finally retreated, exhausted by the fighting and the forced march that had preceded it. Tostig was also killed and when he saw the body of his brother, Harold was so enraged that he cut off his head. He had won. Against a promise never to return, Harold allowed Olaf, the son of the King of Norway, to return home with the survivors who were so few that 24 ships were enough to carry them.

Still in ignorance of the Norwegian disaster, William had in the meanwhile heard of Hardrada's entry into York and also knew the Harold, the usurper of the English throne had set off to encounter him. Accompanied by 25 knights, William undertook to reconnoitre a way to get his army through the marshes which surrounded Pevensey. His aim was to get to Hastings where he could fortify a position more favourable than Anderida, before marching on London. The chargers, however, got bogged down and their riders had to lead them back to Pevensey. The searing heat of the season, which had cost the Norwegians dear, was also having its effect there, so much so that the knights struggled out of their coats of mail and carried them over their shoulders. Very soon though, William Fitz-Osborn, Lord of Crépon and one of the Bastard's followers and closest friend could no longer shoulder the burden that was throwing him off balance. Thus William, with a laugh, took the mail coat and put it on top of his own. He was a man of uncommon strength and endurance.

Hastings

The Normans only remained for one night at Pevensey, the time strictly necessary to reorganise the army after the difficulties of the crossing.

When they left ancient Anderida, the warriors had to go round the bay, a distance of more than 40 km. via the west and the north. Roads were rare and involved long detours. William passed through the hamlet of Wartling, marched north of Ninfield, Catsfield and Crowhurst, passing south of Caldbec Hill, little doubting that two weeks later his destiny would be decided at that very place. There he reached a crossroads, on the one side Dover and on the other an ancient road that joined London to Lewes, while to the south lay the only road to Hastings on the slopes of Telham Hill.

The rear echelon people did not follow behind. While the cavalry and infantry were pillaging the countryside a sufficient number of vessels had again put to sea loaded with the necessities for re-supply and fortification. The carpenters watched over their precious loads : enormous baulks of timber destined for provisional fortifications, rather like a child's gigantic construction kit but made up of prefabricated elements in oak and chestnut which could be assembled in various ways so as to make best use of the configuration of a site for its defence.

Whichever route was taken the entire force gained the Hastings peninsula where also the coast was indented. The sea had got in behind a long tongue of land which held back the water from the network of streams running in from the north to form the lagoon of Bulverhythe. Hastings was both a town and a port but both today have disappeared under either sand or water, replaced by newer structures and the ancient lagoon has had luxury hotels built on it.

Hastings possesses a prominent cliff which towers above to the

Note the metal tipped wooden spades of uneven shape.

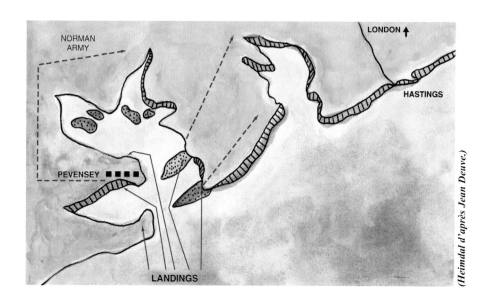

(Heimdal d'après Jean Deuve.)

tune of several dozens of metres and which had been settled by the Celts. Among the ancient ruins the Saxons had built a church and a fortified settlement. It was there, on the clifftop that William ordered his brother Robert, Count of Mortain, to construct a motte (artificial earth mound) with a wooden castle on top according to Norman custom and depicted in the Bayeux tapestry. Later, this early structure was replaced by one with solid stone walls, of which the imposing ruins can still be seen today.

A Saxon nobleman observed the preparations and leapt on his horse to warn Harold.
A knight of that country
Heard the noise and the cries
Of the local people
Seeing the fleet straight ahead.
He knew that the Normans were coming
And that it was his land they wanted.
On top of a hill he observed,
Hidden so as not to be seen,
He looked and saw
How the great fleet arrived.
Quickly the archers disembarked
Followed by the knights,
The carpenters with their axes.
The nobles with their retinues.
Quickly the timbers were unloaded
And quickly the camp was fortified
And a ditch dug around it.
Quickly the shields and weapons were brought in.
When he seen everything,
He took his lance and sword:
To King Harold he went
To tell him his news.
So he set off,
Retiring late and rising early
Night and Day he galloped
To find Harold his King.
Beyond the Humber he found him,
In a town where he was dining.
He said to him "the Normans have come,
To Hastings where they have landed,
And will take England from you,
If you do not defend it.
There they have built a castle
Embellished with towers and a ditch".

Rou. Verses 6617 to 6650.

The Hastings plateau sloped gently down to the north. Very narrow at one point it formed a sort of peninsula and it was there that William decided to establish his military base before setting out to conquer London. In effect William was protected to the west by the Bulverhythe lagoon and to the East by the marshes of the rivers Brede and Rother on either side of the village of Sedlescombe. To the north-west lay the extensive swampy forest of the Andredsweald, perfect for delaying the advance of the Saxon army.

Both for the Normans and the Saxons the best road to London was the northerly one which linked Dover and Southwark via Canterbury and Rochester, because the old Roman road through Andredsweald was to dilapidated to allow a movement through hostile territory. William could have marched to London to make himself master of the city before the return of the Saxon army but he courted the risk of having his retreat cut off and being besieged in the Hastings peninsula he was safe although he realised that he could not stay there. He had in effect only one course open to him — to meet Harold as soon as he found himself facing him, which was to occur shortly.

While his men perfected their defences, he sent out his detachments to bring in supplies. In the surrounding villages there were terror raids, cattle round-ups and burnings. Apart from being an easy source of booty, the victuals taken from the local population and the clearance of a security zone had a wider strategic purpose which became more and more obvious from day to day, acting as it did by creating a climate of insecurity, demonstrating to the inhabitants that the Normans were now the masters. Those responsible for protecting them and their goods were notable by their absence. It was remarkable that the systematic pillage, which had been forbidden at the beginning of the campaign in Normandy and Ponthieu, was encouraged by the Duke. It was a normal part of all feudal wars which William did not fail to apply as it was the best way to attract Harold to confront him for a final confrontation.

William finally heard about the defeat at Stamford Bridge, the news having been brought by

the seneschal of the late King, Edward the Confessor - by means of a letter, Robert Fitz-Wimarch also told him that Harold had left for Hastings. The latter had heard of the Norman landing on 2 October, while he was treating the wounds of his army after the victory over the Norwegians, a battle which had been won, but at a terrible price. He could not hope to make up his numbers locally in view of the sympathy shown to the invaders by the inhabitants of York. He would have to rely on the fyrd of his own earldom, Wessex which stretched from Kent to Cornwall (which would take time to assemble) as well as a few recruits collected on the way from York to London. He put is two remaining brothers, Gyrth and Lewine, earls of East Anglia and Essex, in charge of enrolling as many as possible to encounter William. Harold left for London which he reached on **6 October,** without, however, the brothers Edwin of Mercia and Morcar of Northumberland nor any thegns (noblemen) from their earldoms.

Robert Fitz-Wimarch took the liberty of advising William not to seek battle but rather to stay inside his fortifications. According to the former, Harold's power was enormous, enabling him to kill the invincible Harold Hardrada, and that the Bastard would

not be able to overcome him. The Duke's reply was not long in coming. *"Tell your Lord,"* he said to the messenger, *"I would rather have had a letter of a different kind. I have no intention of cowering behind my fortifications and intend to give battle at the first opportunity. to the usurper of the throne of England which is mine by right. Even if I have six times less men, I will crush Harold".*

Discounting the final swaggering remark, William was right. Having often beaten his enemies by besieging them, he knew only too well the futility of hiding behind walls, however strong they might be which was far from being the case at Hastings. Such a course implied a progressive deterioration, hunger, an undignified surrender and finally, death. In this respect he was ignoring the three years resistance put up by his treacherous cousin, Guy of Burgundy, behind his walls at Brionne.

Ambassadors succeede one another; On arrival in London, Harold sent a monk who arrived at Hastings wile William was carrying out an inspection of his fleet, beached below the cliffs. The Duke greeted the emissary of the King of England without disclosing who he was.

He pretended that the Duke was absent and that he was his se-

neschal and chief advisor. "Tell me the tenor of the message and I will see that he gets it" he said to the monk.

"King Harold says that he remembers perfectly well that King Edward intended that the Duke should inherit the kingdom. King Harold admits that he went to Normandy to confirm the succession, but then his discovered that Kind Edward on is deathbed, had changed his mind. King Harold demands that William return to his lands in Normandy with his soldiers — if not, he will revoke any past agreements."

The false seneschal shook his head. The following day he received the monk at his court, dressed in his finest clothes and flanked by his brothers Robert and Odo as well as Geoffrey de Montbray, Bishop of Coutances. When he recognised the Duke of Normandy the messenger was stupefied.

"This", said the Duke, *"is Huon Margot, a monk like you who comes from my abbey at Fécamp and speaks your language. He will carry my reply to the man you serve."* Margot was evidently one of William's spies, once a monk from an English abbey that was under the supervision of Fécamp. This was how Wace told the story :

*The Duke was well aware
That Harold had returned from
the North*

And that Tostig, his brother, was dead.
Huon Margot said of himself,
That he was tonsured monk from Fécamp.
That he had been well educated,
Was wise and well regarded.
The Duke sent him to Harold.
And Margot set off.
He found Harold in London
And it was there that he spoke to him.

Rou. Verses 6753 to 6763.

Margot made the following speech :

"It is without foolhardiness not to cause offence to justice , but upon reflection and within my rights that I have arrived in a country inherited from my cousin, King Edward, in return for all the favours he received both from my father and myself. At the time he judged me to be the most suitable to rule his kingdom after his death, just as I had helped him during his lifetime. Archbishop Stigand and the Earls, Godwin of Wessex, Leofric of Mercia and Siward of Northumberland who took an oath to recognise me, swearing not to oppose my coming to the throne, approved this choice. Harold swore loyalty to me and promised me the kingdom. If he wishes I will plead my case according to English or Norman law, at his convenience. If he refuses, to preserve the lives of his soldiers and mine, I am ready to meet him in single combat to defend my right to the throne of England."

At those words, Harold went as white as a sheet and was silent for a long time, bewildered, but at last he mumbled :

"We will also mobilise. We will march into battle".

Huon Margot insisted that the Duke did not want the destruction of the two armies. He wanted a single-combat.

Harold looked up at the ceiling and replied :

"Whoever the Lord judges to be in the right, William or me, that is his right."

Harold got his army on the road, leaving London on 11 October. According to Wace, Huon Margot was threatened with death by Harold but saved at the last

moment by the intervention of the latter's brother, Gyrth. Thus Harold sent him back to William with orders to state that his oath to the Duke had been made under duress, and only to be able to escape, thus in his eyes it was invalid. If he, William, re-embarked for Normandy, Harold would help him with a goodly sum of money. If not they would fight.

Odo of Bayeux, Duke William and Robert, Count of Mortain.

Duke William replied :

For your words I thank you,
But I did not come here
With so many shields,
To hear such pleas,
But rather to have all the land
That was promised to me
And which Edward gave to me
Together with hostages,
Two children of the highest lineage.

Rou. Verses 6847 to 6856.

Following on those exchanges via emissaries, confusion reigned within the royal family. Gyrth, the younger of Harold's brothers, tried to persuade him to let him, Gyrth, fight in his place, because he had never sworn anything to William and thus would not be breaking an oath, thus he could command the troops. Harold would only have to await the result of the battle without participating in person.

Their mother, Gytha intervened by reproaching Harold for the death of Tostig and she wanted to make sure that the other brothers stayed alive. Then Gyrth joined in again by telling Harold that he should order the devastation of all the countryside around Hastings, to gain time, swell the ranks of the army and starve out the Normans before the onset of winter. Harold rejected that course out of hand, saying that he would not make his own people suffer on account of the conflict. What he did do, though, was to send out his fleet to cruise along the south coast to cut off the invaders' retreat.

During the afternoon of **13** October, the Saxons halted as they emerged from the forest , on Caldbec Hill where Harold established his headquarters about a kilometre from the edge of the Andredsweald at a place known as the Hoar Apple Tree. There the roads to London, Rochester and Dover, Chichester and Lewes met, woith Hastings 12km. to the south. Harold intended to re-use the tactic employed against Hardrada, catching the Normans by surprise and crushing them in the same way, preferably at night. If that failed he would bottle them up in the Hastings peninsula at sea and by land until his reinforcements arrived.

He had hardly any more men than when he left York and the Earls, Edwin and Morcar had hardly sent him anyone. On the road south, peasants had been more or less forcibly recruited into the ranks of the fyrd and hastily armed with spears and sticks into which a sharp stone had been inserted — that type of weapon was known by the Danish as a *Morgenstern*, (in English, a mace), but such men could only be regarded as auxiliaries. When mobilised the men of the southern counties fyrd moved through the countryside and the ecclesiastical contingent was not negligible. The abbeys of Winchester and Peterborough furnished strong contingents, as well as monks!

On both sides the intelligence services were busy, and the Norman scouts galloped ceaselessly between the Saxon front and the Norman fortress, which negated the effect of surprise counted on by Harold and caused William to place his troops on alert.

Two Saxon spies were caught and taken before William, but instead of hanging them on the spot, he took his guests for a walk through the Norman camp established to the north of Hastings on Baldslow Ridge, gave them food and drink and then sent them back to their base. On arrival back at the Hoar Apple tree they were taken to Harold's headquarters to whom they gave a detailed report of their mission, telling him about the discipline and extraordinary deployment of the Norman army. One of the two, however, who was not terribly intelligent, imagined that all he had seen was an armymade up of clerics, because all of William's men were clean shaven and had short hair. This was how Wace described it :

One of the English who had seen
The Normans clean shaven and
with short haircuts.
Believed that they were all
priests
Only good for saying prayers,
All short haired
And without moustaches under
their noses.
He said to Harold that William
That Harold had more clerics in
his lands
Then knights or other men.
He was astonished
That all were clean shaven.
But Harold replied
That they were brave knights.
Hardy and good fighters.
"They have neither moustaches
nor shaggy hair,"
Harold told him, "as we have."

Rou. Verses 7095 to 7110.

Having two years earlier accompanied the Duke of Normandy on his campaign to restore order in Brittany, the Earl of Wessex was well aware of the military effectiveness of those supposed clerics!

The night fell on two excited armies. The Norman chroniclers liked to pretend that the "French" went to sleep after meditation and prayer, while the Saxons spent the evening feasting and

drinking, a version that in difficult to credit taking into account their forced march from London after fighting two battles in two weeks, as well as what was at stake during the day to come.

Still according to Wace, Harold was gripped by fear when he realised the strength of the Norman forces and wanted to return to London to collect reinforcements :

"I want to return to London
To collect more soldiers".
"Harold", said Gyrth, Ôrotten coward!
It is too late for that.
It would have been better to
think about that earlier,
Before launching us on this cavalcade.
Rotten coward! When I tell you
That the nobles begged you
strongly
When you were staying in London,
To let me fight instead,
You did not want to agree
And did the contrary."

Rou. Verses 7017 to 7028.

One can bet that Wace was exaggerating as such a reaction was totally contrary to the character of Harold who was certainly no coward. Even if it is probable that did regret not having taken the time to properly assemble his forces, one cannot reasonably admit a desire on his part to retreat when the two armies were face to face.

In fact in both camps, nobody was in any doubt that 14 October 1066, the day of Saint Calixtus, would be that of the decisive confrontation.

Getting ready for the battle – shields, arrows, padded tunics and jerkins. Photo taken at Battle in October 2000. (G.B.)

The fighting man in 1066

Civilian Clothing

Thanks to the Bayeux Tapestry and sundry archaeological finds it is possible to form a pretty good idea of the clothing and equipment of both the Saxons and the Normans who fought at Hastings. But there remain a number of unanswered questions concerning various details.

Most wore a shirt, trousers and stockings, and over those garments a man wore a linen tunic or jerkin, the collar of which had a slight opening at the front to ease pulling it over the head. A strip of different coloured cloth often surrounded that opening and the collar itself and the tunic were gathered up at the waist by a leather belt. The tunic's skirt was often slit in four places, back front and at the sides. This enabled one to lift up these panels and tuck them into the belt, which was useful when marching barelegged in water or when disembarking from a boat as can be seen in the Tapestry. Some men seem to have worn short linen knee-length trousers with their stockings underneath.

The stockings could have strips of cloth wound around them like puttees and leather shoes were worn on the feet. Even though not seen on the Tapestry, soldiers could wear a linen hood, which covered the shoulders and kept the head warm, a very practical garment.. A linen cape that could be fastened to the chest or the right shoulder was favoured by the cavalry.

All these garments were dyed in natural colours, mainly brown or beige, but also red, green or blue, although the latter three were reserved for members of the nobility.

The Normans and the men of Picardy in the 11th century were clean-shaven and their necks were shaved as is shown in this extract from the Bayeux Tapestry (below).

This contingent are not shaved quite to high up (above). In fact though, this form of tonsure went much higher up the back of the head as is shown in the Tapestry.

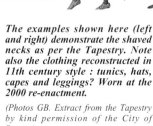

The examples shown here (left and right) demonstrate the shaved necks as per the Tapestry. Note also the clothing reconstructed in 11th century style : tunics, hats, capes and leggings? Worn at the 2000 re-enactment.

(Photos GB. Extract from the Tapestry by kind permission of the City of Bayeux).

Hairstyles and moustaches

The Tapestry gives us interesting indications of the fashions of that period which allow us to distinguish the participants.

The Norman cavalry were always presented as being beardless, with short hair and with their necks shaven, a style that was practical for mounted men whose heads were enclosed by the mail hood under their conical helmets. Any superfluous hair would have been a nuisance and it was military dress which dictated the fashion. This can be confirmed by observing the labourers when the stores were being embarked and in the camp at Hastings who did not have the napes of their necks shaven. Those who did were Guy, Count of Ponthieu, Duke William and his suite.

Many of the Saxons, at least the nobles, wore a moustache and half long hair. That was the case with the moustaches of Harold and his brother Gyrth, but not of his other brother, Leowine.

Let us now consider the military accoutrements worn over the clothing.

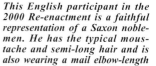

This English participant in the 2000 Re-enactment is a faithful representation of a Saxon noblemen. He has the typical moustache and semi-long hair and is also wearing a mail elbow-length hauberk which came down to the knees – a Norman-style pattern. Compare him with the Tapestry extract (left) showing Harold arriving at Bosham with his suite. On the other hand, Harold's army included Anglo-Danish contingents from north east England like these Danes (left). The other photo (below) shows an example of the Saxon army – one of the soldiers is carrying a long-handled battleaxe. (photos taken at Hastings 2000 by GB. Extract from the Tapestry courtesy of the City of Bayeux).

1

2

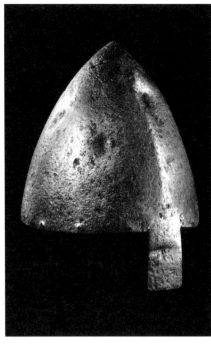

3

Helmets

The many examples illustrated in the Bayeux Tapestry feature conical helmets with nose guards. The conical part was generally made of several pieces of metal, probably four, riveted together. This cone was fixed to an iron band, which fitted round the head and held the whole thing together. The nose guard was a prolongation of this designed to protect the nose and face from sword cuts. It has been generally considered that these designs consisted of a metal structure: headband with nose guard and four cruciform uprights joined at the top. This assumption is probably correct as such a system would provide great rigidity and could easily be mass-produced which was necessary for equipping thousands of men. On the other hand, given the price of metal at the time, and using this method of construction, the simple soldiers could be equipped with helmets made up from the same cruciform metal framework with nose guard and the four infill pieces could have been of leather. This type was called a banded helmet and was the direct successor to the helmets used in northern Europe between the 8th and 10th centuries, of which several examples have been unearthed during archaeological excavations, mainly dating from the Viking period. It is logical to see its successor on the heads of Normans and Saxons.

At the same time, in central Europe, helmets with nose guards forged from a single sheet of metal were in use. An example is the helmet of St. Wenceslas, dating from the 10th century and preserved in the treasury of Prague cathedral. It consists of the conical part, lightly ribbed and forged from a single sheet, embellished with a circular strip of metal bearing decorations in silver, which were of the north European pattern and continued down onto the nose guard. Another type of helmet with nose guard forged from a single piece was discovered in 1864 in the presbytery at Olmutz in the Czech Republic. It dated from the 11th century, was forged from a single piece of metal and lacked any decorative embellishments although lightly ribbed. Small holed round the base and a light hook behind the nose guard served to attach the helmet lining, which is preserved in the weapons collection of the History of Art Museum in Vienna. In his book, Laking (p.44 et seq.) has compared sixteen conical helmets of the period. In closely examining the Bayeux Tapestry, there is at least one helmet which appears to have been forged from a single piece of metal. Given the patterns of trade at that time and the diverse origins of the combatants, it would appear that the riveted helmet was the norm although forged ones were also present on the heads of some of those who fought at Hastings. These two types were still being worn into the following century and the conical helmet with nose guard remained the standard until circa 1200.

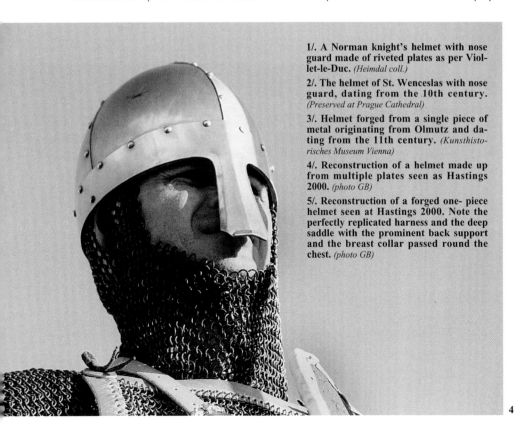

1/. A Norman knight's helmet with nose guard made of riveted plates as per Viollet-le-Duc. *(Heimdal coll.)*

2/. The helmet of St. Wenceslas with nose guard, dating from the 10th century. *(Preserved at Prague Cathedral)*

3/. Helmet forged from a single piece of metal originating from Olmutz and dating from the 11th century. *(Kunsthistorisches Museum Vienna)*

4/. Reconstruction of a helmet made up from multiple plates seen as Hastings 2000. *(photo GB)*

5/. Reconstruction of a forged one-piece helmet seen at Hastings 2000. Note the perfectly replicated harness and the deep saddle with the prominent back support and the breast collar passed round the chest. *(photo GB)*

4

5

On this extract from the Tapestry we can see Harold and his suite in discussion with Guy of Ponthieu : their sword belts hang down on each side of their swords and the scabbards are fitted in a metal slide. (Courtesy of City of Bayeux)

Swords

The patterns used at the time are well-known thanks to the numerous examples which have been preserved or found from excavations. At that time they used a straight sword with a long blade (total length a little over 90 cm.) having two cutting edges with a central groove and a gently rounded tip. Such a weapon was used to cut rather than to stab with the point. It was the direct descendant of the huge Carolingian swords and only the shape of the guard or the pommel varied.

This long sword was still the sort used by the Carolingian warriors or the Vikings, but in the 11th century there was a technical development. According to Edward Salin is his Civilisation Mérovingienne (vol III, p. 107) the damascened sword disappeared: "at about this time and as a result of the progress achieved by defensive weapons, the numerous welds involved in their manufacture were a source of inferiority

and they were replaced by weapons made with different techniques."

The numerous examples illustrated in the Bayeux Tapestry show many variations in the length of the guards. The Carolingian or Viking type of sword had short guards, the tips of which did not protrude very far. That type of guard did not give much protection to the hands against sword cuts, and one can also see models with much longer straight guards, a type which established itself in the 12th century. The sword worn by Guy of Ponthieu as seen on the Tapestry is of this type. There also exist several inward-curved guards, which had already appeared during the 10th century especially in the Scandinavian areas, either curved down towards the blade or upward towards the pommel (there are a few rare examples on the Tapestry).

It is difficult to make out the shape of the pommels but several examples are in existence. They were often in the form of pyramids, especially the models with straight guards, or lozenge-shaped.

Scabbards were made of leather, covering perhaps two strips of wood. At that time they had not discovered the baldrick or shoulder belt and the sword was attached to the left hand side of the waist-belt and the Tapestry shows in detail how it was fastened on. When Harold as a prisoner, was talking to Guy of Ponthieu, one can see that several of the Saxons and Harold himself had removed their swords, to leave the belt hanging down on each side. The scabbard was passed through a metal frog fixed directly onto the belt.

In battle the belt was worn under the hauberk with only the point sticking out below the hem. Sometimes though, the sword was worn outside and a slit in the hauberk, level with the frog made this possible.

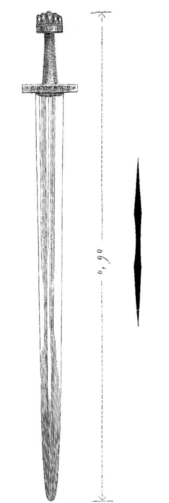

Carolingian type sword drawn by Viollet-le-Duc, 90cm long from the tip of the blade to the pommel. A shows a cross-section of the blade.

Damascened sword from the Denon Museum at Chalon, a technique that disappeared during the 11th century.

A different Carolingian sword from the Denon Museum.

Swordsmanship training at Hastings 2000. (photo GB)

Different types of sword drawn by Viollet-le-Duc and taken from the Tapestry. A is still the Carolingian type while B is a new design with longer guards.

In the Book of Devotions of Otto III one of the men of the emperor's suite is wearing a typical 11th century sword with long guards. This type continued in use during the following century. (Staatsbibliothek, Munich)

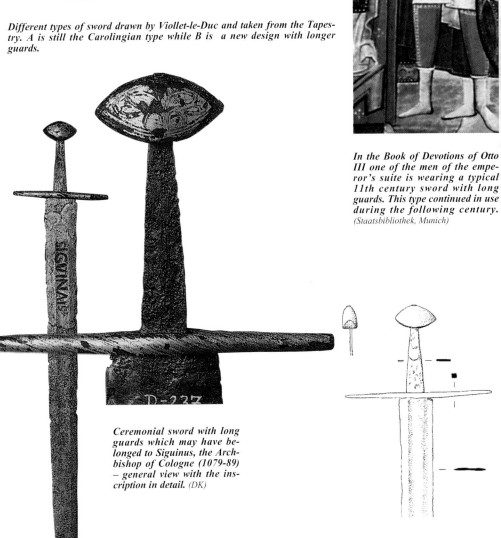

11th century sword with pyramidal pommel and two short straight guards, auctioned by Maitre Bisman at Rouen on 20 June 1999. (photo E Bruneval/MA)

Ceremonial sword with long guards which may have belonged to Siguinus, the Archbishop of Cologne (1079-89) – general view with the inscription in detail. (DK)

A sword from the Douai Museum with long guards and almond-shaped pommel, identical to the two previous examples.

(S.B.)

Shields

At least since the 5th century the Germanic shield had been round with a central metallic boss, a metal band around the outside and covered with leather. Various examples have survived including a Scandinavian one, which still has the majority of the wooden strips from which it was constructed held together with tongue and groove joints. These round shields were flat and offered a high degree of protection if the wearer understood how to move it quickly to parry blows, but offered less protection than the Norman kite-shaped shield. The Saxons at Hastings seem to have partially adopted the latter style although the round shield remained in use as can be seen in the Tapestry. Conservatism perhaps? Some of the round shields shown there, appear to have a cambered surface but that may well be a stylistic convention to emphasis the shield of a fighter seen in profile.

The Normans were equipped with kite-shaped shields known as the Norman shield. According to Viollet-le-Duc their shields were 1.30 m. high and circa 0,56 m. at their widest part. Pointed at the base they were finished off at the top in the form of a semi-circle. They were made of various perishable materials, wood, leather and various metal elements, none of which have survived. In the centre of the shield there was a small metal boss,

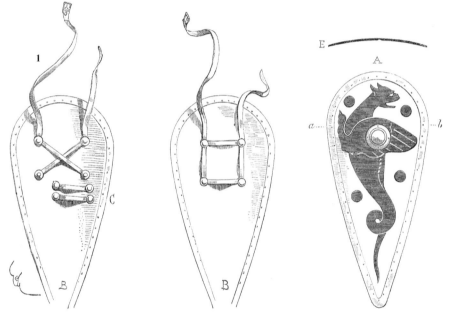

1/. Based on details shown in the Tapestry, Viollet-le-Duc drew the leather arm straps which enabled a horseman to hold his kite-shaped shield in various positions.

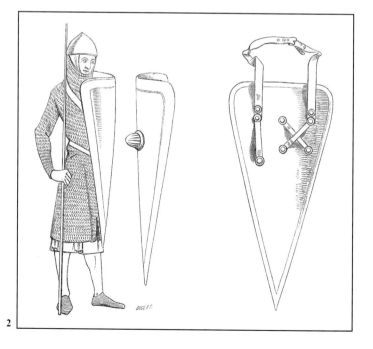

2/. Still as per Viollet-le-Duc this was the system used a century and a half later circa 1200. 2

partly to reinforce it and partly to deflect blows. Strips of leather fixed on with nails reinforced the edges.

As opposed to the round shield, the kite-shaped ones were slightly concave which afforded extra protection for the body and the left leg of a cavalryman. On the other hand from what we know of kite-shaped shields of the 12th and early 13th century, they had a much more pronounced curve. Why did this innovation have to wait until the following century? These shields, like the round ones, were made up from jointed wooden slats, like the staves of a barrel, stuck together and reinforced by glue made from animal skins. That sort of glue, still used until comparatively recently allowed an extremely satisfactory result and afforded great rigidity. The leather covering of the shield, stuck on with the same glue also contributed to the rigidity.

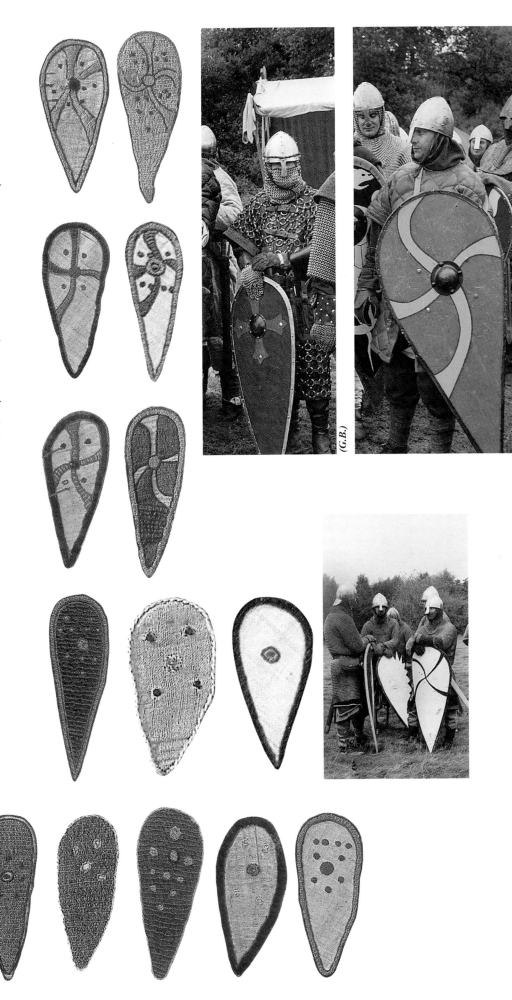

(G.B.)

(G.B.)

Certain shields from the early middle Ages have survived down to our times. The oldest one is the Seedorf shield, originating at the abbey of the same name founded in 1197, and the shield itself dates from circa 1200. It is made of wood and leather covered which is continued on over the back. It is decorated with a lion in silver on a blue background, which was the armorial emblem of Arnold of Brienz who was the founder of the abbey and who died in 1225. It is in the Norman shape but has been cut down at the top end to bring it into line with the fashion of circa 1220. It measures 87 cm long with the point missing and has a maximum width of 67 cm. All these shields are wooden, mainly linden wood and between 7 and 15 mm thick. They were covered with leather and often had a leather border although never in metal. The height of these "Norman shields" depended on the height of the user and is estimated on average to have been circa 1.20 m.

On the inside the arm straps provided a strong grip enabling the shield to be firmly held in several positions. Two methods were employed both equally practical, described as follow by Viollet-le-Duc (French 19th century antiquarian and architectural historian. Trans.). "The carrying device consisted of four straps forming a square, in such a way that the shield could be held vertically if one passed one's arm through them, and horizontally if one passed the arm through on the main axis. The long strap, which enabled the shield to be slung from the shoulder, was fixed to the top by two rivets as is shown in the illustration. In some cases the carrying straps were fixed in the form of a cross with two straps hanging down underneath. The arm was passed through the latter and the hand grabbed the cross as in figure C." The interior of those shields was padded, which also acted as reinforcement.

Decoration was extremely diverse and the Bayeux Tapestry provides several examples, which can broadly be classified into three categories:

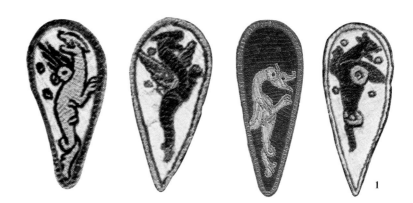

1/. Various forms of dragons painted on Norman shields, according to the Bayeux Tapestry

2/. The Seedorf shield dating from circa 1200 is probably the only one existing of the so-called Norman pattern. ; the rounded upper part was cut off circa 1220 to bring it into line with the fashion of the time. It is made of wood covered in leather. *(Swiss national Museum, Zurich)*

3/. Round shields were used throughout the early middle ages until around the year 1000 but some peoples; notably the Saxons, retained them until 1066. *(University Museum of National Antiquities, Oslo).*

- Short crosses or wavy lines spread over the whole length of the shield. The latter were more common.

- Dragons were also common with wings and serpent tails. They could be facing either left or right and their heads were turned backwards facing their wings.

- Geometric patters were also popular. One common motive consisted of coloured spots spread symmetrically over a background of a different colour. The rivet heads that attached the carrying straps to the back of the shield and were visible on the outside surface may well have inspired this design. Might this well have been symbolic, the number of coloured spots defi-

ning a particular unit? It is impossible to say. One can also see a number the tri-coloured shields, the background being of one colour, the border in another and the boss in a third. The latter was absent from other shields, which were in two colours. Another type, which was quite rare, featured a serrated pattern around the edge.

All the colours used were natural pigments, which were not as vi-

vid as modern paints: white, beige, brown, red and green, usually on white backgrounds. The designs did not represent personal arms, the earliest of which was the blazon of Geoffroy le Bel, dating from the middle of the 12th century. During the Norman period, the patters used were seemingly at random, but were they, before the battle, a recognition sign for a unit or simply a matter of personal

Shields were made of wood and covered with leather and the kite-shaped Norman ones were slightly concave. They were formed from strips of wood jointed together like barrel staves. The animal skin based glue and the leather covering provided rigidity as did the arm straps at the back. Here is the outline of a reconstructed shield which are normally made from lime tree wood.

(G.B.)

(E.G.)

Lances

The lances used by the Normans were fitted with two different types of tip. According to Viollet-le-Duc, one had two barbs while the other sort was leaf-shaped (see illustration below). This was essentially the weapon of the cavalry and signified the rider's status but was also used by the infantry. It was light enough to be used as a spear but could also be thrown like a javelin. In the Bayeux Tapestry one can them flying though the air, embedded in shields or stuck in the ground. A different type was the long lance of the cavalry, tucked under the arm, the formidable shock weapon of the Norman cavalry, sometimes fitted with a pennant, as we shall see later.

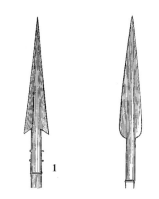

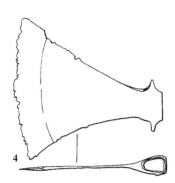

Lances were first and foremost a cavalry weapon. According to Viollet-le-Duc, (1) the Norman lance had two different shapes of blade. It could also be used as a javelin being held towards the base of the shaft as in (2) taken by Viollet-le-Duc from the Tapestry. The long lance carried tucked under the army was used as a shock weapon. The photo (3) illustrates an attack by Norman cavalry against Saxon infantry (Assor). As for the Saxons they used the great battleaxe with a broad blade inherited from the Vikings (4); (drawing based on archaeological evidence).

Battleaxes

Axes were an infantry weapon, much used by the Vikings in combination with the sword - mainly the long-handled axe that had a devastating effect when wielded in an arc in front of the body. Essentially it was a shock weapon for forcing a way through en enemy line and could also be used as a combination weapon. Thanks to its slightly curved blade, an infantryman could hack into the shield of an opponent and pull it away from him, while another man could spear him in the side. The "Saxons" against the "Normans" used this tactic during the re-enactment of the Battle of Hastings in 14 October 2000. The large battleaxe was mainly used by the Saxons and in the Bayeux Tapestry, Leowine, one of Harold's brothers, was brandishing one as he was cut down and killed by the Normans. The territories of Earl Morcar in the northeast of England were very much an Anglo-Danish area marked by a strong Viking influence having been colonised by the latter. Thus it was quite normal that the battleaxe, essentially a Scandinavian weapon, was common in Harold's army. On the other hand, the Norman infantry may well have been equipped with them as well, as was indicated in the scene in the Tapestry of the embarkation of stores, showing a soldier carrying an axe. (see above)

Hauberks and Jerkins

The hauberk was the name given to the long coat of chain mail worn essentially by the cavalry while the broigne was a leather jerkin to which metal pieces were sewn to give added protection.

Did the Norman cavalry wear hauberks or leather jerkins? In his definitive Dictionaire de Mobilier (Dictionary of Equipment) (vol. 5, pp.70 - 73 & 241 - 242), Violet-le-Duc opts for the second solution. On the Bayeux Tapestry those coats often had a trellis pattern or appeared to be strengthened by metal plates in-

dicated in the form of small circles. One can assume from an examination of the tapestry that those circles represented mail links. However, other testimony from the same era, executed with greater care for detail, permit us to see that these circles were nothing more than metal rings sewn onto a leather or cloth coat, doubled over and padded. Colonel Penguilly d'Haridon in his catalogue of the Artillery Museum has rightly made the distinction between the coat of mail and the leather or cloth coat fitted with metal rings. ; it does not appear that mail coats or hauberks were adopted in France until the 12th century and during the first half of the latter they remained relatively rare." He then offered a reconstruction of a Norman knight (see illustration overleaf) who is wearing a long leather jerkin onto which metal rings have been fixed.

It is true that in the graphic style of the Tapestry, the combat clothing worn by the knights does not permit any firm conclusions to be drawn. However, according to archaeological discoveries, Viking chieftains did wear mail coats. Therefore why not in Normandy or northern England? Moreover, there is evidence of the wearing of chain mail by knights in a period prior to that indicated by Viollet-le-Duc, notably on a fine bas-relief on the façade of Angoulème cathedral dated at circa 1100.

1

1/. Viollet-le-Duc was the first to have studied closely the equipment of the Norman cavalry in 1066, and in 1874 addressed the problem. The only source of information was the Bayeux Tapestry which is accurate but stylised and he presented various problems some of which have still not been resolved – the leather jerkins covered with metal plates or rings as in the drawing on the left (1) or the mail hauberk. The latter had been in existence for quite some time although only used by the wealthier knights. The jerkins covered in round or square plates were also worn as evidenced by the Tapestry.

2/. Another problem discussed by le-Duc concerned the neck opening of the hauberk with a rectangular flap edged with leather at the base of the neck. Viollet-le-Duc suggested the design seen at "A" with the comment : "this jerkin was a short sleeved tunic. (…..) It was necessary to pass it over the body through a rectangular opening at the top, closed off by a flap fastened by four buttons. At the back, "B" that mail hood hung down. opening at the top

3/. & 4/. These reconstructions suggest how the flap was used. (photo GB at Hastings 2000).

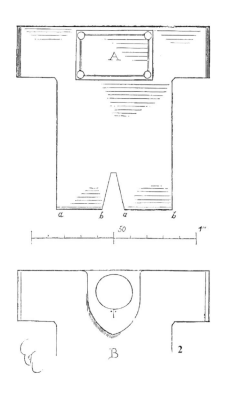

2

Thus the wearing of chain mail hauberks was apparent much earlier and spread throughout the first thousand years of our epoch in northern Europe, including the Viking era. The large hauberks of the Norman knights and the Saxon elite troops were, according to available evidence, a garment that was both supple and practical in combat

One should not forget that other protective garments were worn at the same time, notably the long leather jerkins or shirts onto which metal rings or plates could be attached. The excavations at the chateau at Blois have uncovered such a plate dating from the 9th or 10th century which included the remains of a rivet. Three holes can be seen on the border of this plate, which is some 6 cm. in diameter. At Colletière at another site from the same period various jerkin plates have been found but no vestiges of mail.

Thus it appears the leading personalities, both Norman and Saxon, were equipped with the long chain mail hauberk. However, the number of participants

3

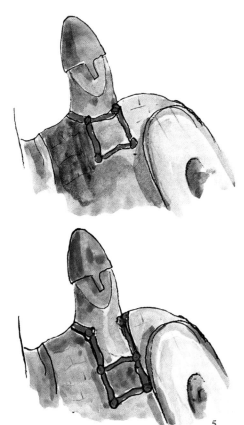

5/. These set of drawings represent two systems for the neck opening of a hauberk shown on the Tapestry : either a rectangular flap edged with leather fastened with four buttons or a leather band around the neck and a single button. These representations are quite accurate and show more archaic methods than those employed a century later to better protect the neck and chin. (E Groult/Heimdal)

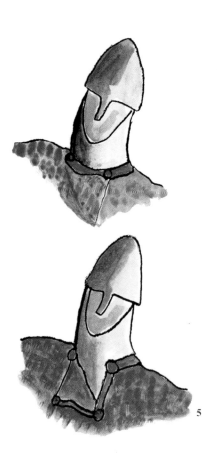

in the battle ran into the thousands, including contingents from Normandy itself, Maine, Brittany, France, Flanders, and each region had its own customs. Apart from the leading nobles and knights, it is probable that the rest of the troops were equipped with the reinforced leather jerkin.

The great hauberk of the Norman knight and the Saxon housecarl (household elite troops), pose other questions. On most examples, one can see at the base of the throat, a mail rectangle edged with leather for which two theories have been advanced : could it have been a mail flap that could be lifted up and attached to the mail hood, to protect the bottom part of the face? In that case however, the wearer would have been unable to breathe, a fact which has been proved by a reconstruction of a costume. This would seem to be a somewhat unrealistic theory.

Viollet-le-Duc and others who have come after him, opted for a simple flap that opened at the top and bottom to enable the wearer to pass his head through the opening. "It consisted of a mail shirt with a wide neck opening, and the opening was protected by this sort of flap". This would appear to be logical especially as in no part of the Tapestry can these flaps be seen covering the face which would be normal in a cavalry charge. Moreover, such flaps are not visible on all the outfits, some of which feature a simple leather border with two buttons at the neckline – possibly another form of opening.

The mail hood could be tightened around the face by a lace which was passed through a leather tube to stop it sliding off during battle and in addition it was held in place by the helmet.

The sleeves of the hauberk came down to the elbows and were hemmed with leather, to leave the lower arms unprotected, while the skirt was slit at the front and back to simplify wearing on horseback.

Based on his interpretations of certain images of the Bayeux Tapestry, Viollet-le Duc concluded that a hauberk covered the thighs in the form of a trouser, but this is contradicted by the images along the borders of the tapestry which show hauberks being pulled up from the base and over the heads of dead combatants, proving that the lower part was in the form of a vented skirt. It is probable that the two flaps of the skirt could be laced together around each thigh to give an appearance of short mail trousers. The bottom edge of the flaps were similarly bordered with leather.

3

1

Certain knights, especially Duke William, had their legs covered in chain mail which consisted of a garment laced up at the back. This was fairly rare, and other than the Duke, few knights were so equipped.

As far as the leather jerkins were concerned, as already mentioned, they came in diverse forms. According to the Tapestry, Bishop Odo of Bayeux was fitted with a jerkin of this type. We have already mentioned the metal reinforcing plates found at Blois and Colletière. There is also the chess set, said to have been Charlemagnes, which was carved in southern Italy, which featured Norman knights from that region in the 11th century, who are wearing jerkins covered with metal scales. There were certainly contingents of Normans from Italy at the Battle of Hastings who would have been equipped in that manner. There would also have been plaited leather jerkins of the type carved on a capital at Vézelay dated at circa 1100, which was the basis of an interesting reconstruction offered by Viollet-le-Duc. Hence the great diversity of clothing of the period. Mail coats were expensive and were reserved for the wealthier knights, those who had a "hauberk fief". We do not know whether or not a gambison, a padded garment, was worn underneath the hauberk or leather jerkin at the time.

2

1/. & 2/. *Jerkins with braided leather strips of a type that can be seen on a capital at Vézelay dating from circa 1100 and reconstructed by Viollet-le-Duc were issued to the majority of the infantry of that epoch. We see here (1) the general aspect of that sort of protective garment worn over a knee-length cloth tunic. The jerkin was reinforced by braided leather strips which can be seen in detail in (2). These were "sewn onto the background leather using leather threads around the twisted thongs or with hempen threads. A skin bonnet covered with a cloth hood protected the head and throat".*

3/. *Leather jerkin with rings sewn onto it as suggested by Viollet-le-Duc (see page 32). This was produced by the Norman company Hag"Dik and it is quite credible that such jerkins existed at the time. The two stylised representations on the Tapestry, round and trellis – suggest that. Such a garment offered as good a protection against sword cuts as a mail hauberk and it war easier to manufacture. A variety of clothing was obviously normal.* (photo GB)

4/. *This knight from the so-called Charlemagne chess set, was carved in southern Italy prior to 1088 for the Norman Duke Robert Guiscard. It could well represent a Norman knight wearing a leather over-jerkin covered with metal scales which gives us another example of the dress of the Norman cavalry. We know that at Hastings there were contingents of Normans who had come from southern Italy who were well aware of the tactics of simulated retreat which was the main cause of the victory in the battle.* (drawing by Viollet-le-Duc from the original piece preserved in the Cabinet des Medailles at the Bibliothèque Nationale, Paris).

5/. *Scene of charging cavalry from the manuscript entitled The Life of St. Edmond dating from between 1125 and 1150 showing Norman Cavalry wearing mail hauberks at a period some sixty years after Hastings.* (Pierpont Morgan Library Ms. 736, New York).

6/. *Knight wearing a mail hauberk and helmet with nose guard in a carving from Angoulème Cathedral circa 1100.* (O Massonaud/ Heimdal)

banner is seen again in much more detail : the cross is ochre or gold, flanked by four blue spots on a white background. For the remaining colours we have to relay on the Tapestry and the excellent reconstructions that have been made. During the first attack by the Norman cavalry, a different banner appears,

Banners

Numerous banners can be seen on the Bayeux Tapestry, the best known being the one given by the Pope to Duke William to sanctify his "crusade" against England. This can be seen three times, the first when it was held by William listening to the report of one of his men at Hastings. It had three points like most of the banners. These were blue and an ochre strip separated them from a white background with a blue surround on the three other sides, on which was an ochre (or gold?) cross. The presence of white and blue is reminiscent of the banner which William bore during his campaign against the Bretons. Was this perhaps his personal one as opposed to the papal banner? It can be seen again a little further on when the Norman cavalry were ready to charge : the blue was replaced by ochre, again possibly gold. Even further, when Duke William was showing himself to prove that he had not been killed, the

different from the others : it features a crow (?) on a semi-circle of white cloth with an ochre border and is the only motive appearing on a banner with the exception of the dragon of Harold and its shape is also unusual. Was it perhaps a Norman banner which had retained the Scandinavian tradition?

One can see other banners being carried by the Norman troops. They are all three-pointed and feature geometric shapes in different colours – stripes, rectangles and coloured spots, in blue, ochre, white red green, grey-green. Some banners had one, two or three spots which may well have signified different cavalry troops or squadrons. This is a strong possibility as otherwise how could one control 7,000 men on the front at Hastings

William's personal banner..
(E.G./Heimdal)

without visible rallying points? Even if we take into account the imagination of the embroiderer the positioning of these banners obviously corresponded to a well defined system and they are quite numerous on the Tapestry which indicates their importance.

There is another banner with a cross on it, carried by the chief of the engineers supervising the construction of wooden fortifications. His colours too were blue, ochre and white.

Saxon banners are less numerous. One can see two which are similar to the Norman ones, except for one of them which has four points/tails. On the other hand, near to Harold there is a man carrying an ensign probably made of boiled leather on which is a red, gold and white dragon. Thus the Saxon red dragon confronted the Norman crow. Other than the dragon there is a mention of another of Harold's banners. Towards the end of the 11th century, the chronicler William of Poitiers, indicated that William the Conqueror, after his coronation, sent Harold's banner to the Pope, "all in material of the finest gold and bearing the image of an armed man".

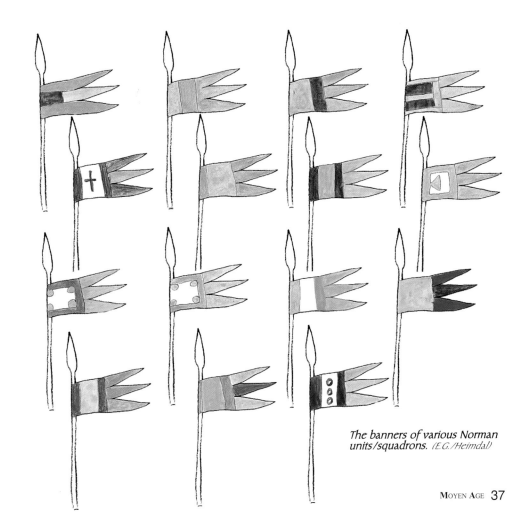

The banners of various Norman units/squadrons. (E.G./Heimdal)

knight had to fit himself out at his own expense, hence the provision of the necessary lands (the hauberk fief) to enable him to defray the costs. A 10th or 11th century stirrup iron found at the chateau of Blois, which was triangular in shape and fitted with a loop through which the stirrup leathers could be threaded. The foot plate was rectangular, 5mm thick and quite wide so as to provide support for the foot when in the thick of battle. Also found in the Blois excavations was a horseshoe with six nail holes, in two of which square cross-section nails were still in place, on average 38 mm long. Another horseshoe had three nail holes on each branch.

The spurs used had a single short conical spike, those found at Blois being 21 and 28 mm in length respectively. Fixing eyes were stamped out on the end of each branch through which were threaded the laces which fastened under the feet and behind the heel. Spurs were made either of forged iron or bronze.

Horses and their harness

The Bayeux Tapestry provides us with many interesting details of the harness used for the horses. The most important item was the saddle, which is easy to see on the Tapestry. It was very deep, fixing the horseman firmly in place between the pommel and the back support which were both prominent. Evidently they were made of wood and covered with leather and enabled the rider to keep his seat even when his lance collided with an enemy. Moreover, a girth went under the horse's belly to fix the saddle firmly to withstand the shock of the charge. The stirrup came into general use in the 8th and 9th centuries, enabling cavalry to dominate the battlefield, and this simple object may well have been the origin of the feudal system. The use of the stirrup made it easier for the horseman to keep himself in the saddle and charge with a lance, thus it was that cavalry became essential for success in battle. A horse and its harness was very costly and a

1/. Forged iron stirrup. (9th/10th century).
2/. Iron horseshoe (end of 10th – early 11th century.
3/. 8th century forged iron spur.
These three objects are preserved in the Museum at Blois.

(photos : Image de Marc, Tours for 1. and 2. S Laroche, MDAVO, for 3.)

The Norman cavalry arm

The Norman knights in the 11th century were the most effective in the whole of Christendom which explains their success in southern Italy and England. At Civitate in 1053 they confronted German knights in the service of Pope Leo IX. The Normans employed their lances whereas the Germans only used swords. According to William of Apulia (vol. II p. 155-60), the Germans "did not understand how to master the movements of their horses and were unable to deliver heavy blows with lances", whereas their opponents were experts in that type of fighting. As the Norman historian Francois Neveu recorded: "the Norman cavalry understood how to manoeuvre and how to charge in a compact group but also how to conduct a strategic retreat by obeying the orders of their commander who generally fought at the head of his knights. This was the case with the Norman leaders at Civitate, notably Richard of Aversa on the right wing, Onfroi in the centre and Robert Guiscard on the left. This was also the case with William at Hastings as can be seen in panel 55 of the Bayeux Tapestry and is born out by the chroniclers, notably William of Poitiers (.....). Regarding the employment of the lance, again the best evidence comes from the

Tapestry. For example in panel 51, we can see that the Normans used three versions. It could be a thrown weapon like a javelin, which was the oldest method or brandished at head height as a spear, the most common in the mid-11th century. Finally the lance could be clamped under the army and intended to hit an adversary hard enough to unseat him, which was to become the technique of the future and established itself during the 12th and 13th centuries as main tournament weapon". (in Les Normands en Mediterranée, Caen University Press, pp 59-59). In no case in Italy were the Normans present in superior numbers. They were always successful against stronger forces because they had mastered the most efficient fighting methods of their era.

To carry our their manoeuvres they organised their cavalry contingents into *conrois*, a term derived from the mediaeval Latin *conredare*, meaning to take care, and were groups of between twenty and thirty horsemen (between a troop and a squadron. Trans.), one of whom was the commander. Such a unit could charge in two ranks and each could be distinguished by a particular banner as can be seen in the Bayeux Tapestry. During the Crusades the armies were subdivided into "battles" which consisted of the equivalent of a dozen conrois. It is evident that, to organise cohesive attacks, simulated retreats and counter-attacks, the alignment in battles and conrois was the key to the Norman success, justly famous for their fighting abilities. On the political level, both in Normandy and Italy, the Norman society was well structured and organised, a model of efficiency for the epoch, and the same factors applied to the cavalry, which was supported by heavy infantry and a corps of archers.

Archers

The bow in use at the time was curved and circa 1.50 m in length and was only flexible at its two extremities. The bowstring attached to the latter was almost at a tangent to the apex. It was made of yew and there was a curved hook made of bone at each end, glued onto the wood and bound with either a silk thread or a gut thing. We know about this type of bow from manuscripts, church carvings and from the numerous details in the Tapestry.

The archers shown there are dressed in light clothing with bonnets on their heads and some are wearing leggings resembling short trousers. Only a few have helmets and mail coats or jerkins.

The crossbow was also in use during that period, one of which was discovered at the Colletière site (Charavines Lake). The stock of a crossbow had been found

intact with a fork at the end for positioning the yew wood bow which still had the traces of the bowstring. The stock was provided with a groove along which the arrow or bolt could slide. The tensioning mechanism pivoted horizontally in a deep groove at the end of the stock. This weapon, already perfected was held in the hand by means of a short spindle. There are no crossbows to be seen on the Tapestry but there is a strong possibility that at least some of the archers at Hastings were equipped with that impressive weapon.

Arrow heads came in various patterns, were often leaf-shaped and made of forged iron.

*1/. **Various forged iron arrow heads, 10th century. Blois Museum.** (Photo : Image de Marc, Tours).*

*2/. **The 11th century short bow, after Viollet-le-Duc.***

*3/. **Reconstruction of an 11th century crossbow found at Colletière The bow is of yew and is fixed to the stock by leather thongs.***

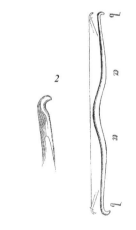

Encampments

It is evident that Duke William's army brought a considerable amount of equipment to England. There is a scene in the Tapestry showing nobles eating a meal at a cloth-covered table whereas the common soldiers used their shields as improvised tables. There are no illustrations showing tents used in the field but two contemporary manuscripts describe the type used in that period : two upright poles were joined by a ridge pole which supported the cloth covering which was pegged into the ground at the base. Various examples have been reconstructed.

Before the Battle

The night attack which Duke William favoured did not take place. The sun rose at around 0530 hours into a clear dawn because the 22 day old moon was entering into its last quarter, spreading its light over the countryside.

The military equipment had been readied for quite some while : the swords had been sharpened and the lance points honed, the arrows and the javelins were ready to fly. The saddle girths had been tightened, as well as the carrying straps on the shields and the chinstraps of the helmets. Men laced up their shoes and wrapped their puttees round their legs after pulling on their breeches. The bulky mail coats and plated jerkins went on last as they were to heavy for wear on the march. 11th century armies had no notion of uniform. The wealthier combatants, the lords and bishops were resplendent in brightly coloured cloth symbolising their riches and high rank : reds, blues and greens edged with embroidery and embellished with jewels.

The majority of the "other ranks" had to be satisfied with neutral colours : ochre, brown or beige, and their decoration was far more modest.

The poorest of the poor were the archers who almost never wore helmets which would have been too heavy for them. Instead they wore a form of cap like a Phrygian bonnet. In addition to his bow and quiver which held circa 25 arrows, the only other arm the archer had was a short sword in a scabbard on the belt, ideal for stabbing, and occasionally a small one-handed axe or hatchet. A tunic of thick linen or padded wool was closed at the collar by a string was worn over the shirt made of thinner linen. He wore leggings with or without feet and wide breeches into which the tunic could be tucked and which came down to the knees like a pair of baggy shorts.

The rest of the infantry generally came from a better off class of society. Their heads were protected by the usual conical helmets with node guards held under the chin by a strap and wore over the top half of their bodies a thick jacked padded out with horsehair. It was made up of several layers of linen stitched together to form ribs that accommodated the stuffing. Over this garment the more fortunate wore a long leather or linen jerkin on which metal plates were sewn to protect against sword cute or even javelin thrusts. Mail hauberks were extremely rare.

Lanes were primarily an infantry weapon, roughly two metres long and held in one hand. In addition, swords were supplied, having an iron guard and a wide channel down the blade. Longer then the Viking swords, they were only drawn during hand to hand combat and were not suitable for stabbing but were used in battle as a cutting weapon.

The kite-shaped shield completed the armament of the Normans. Held on the right it protected the entire body with the exception of the feet. The umbo, the metal semicircular boss that protected the hand of the Viking warrior was no longer indispensable on that type of shield, yet was often present as an added protection against blows or maybe on account of attachment to ancestral tradition.

The horsemen was equipped in the same way and his shield was fitted with four thongs or straps arranged in a square which enabled it to be held upright in any circumstance, mounted or on foot. The wealthier noblemen replaced the leather jerkin with mail over-shirts or hauberks which were more effective but far more costly to procure. To be able to afford them, many did not hesitate to sell their farm in

the hope of rich pickings on the other side of the Channel. The short hauberk came down to the middle of the thighs. Ideal for fighting dismounted, it opened at the front and covered the shoulders. The long hauberk went down over the knees and opened at both front and back. It was the ideal protective garment for knights who were armed with a javelin, lance and sword or mace – the latter having a metal head covered with iron spikes.

Mass was celebrated with due solemnity albeit in somewhat of a hurry, by the two Norman bishops present ; the clean-shaven Odo of Bayeux and the bearded Geoffrey of Coutances who gave communion to the warriors while throughout the army, priests, monks and chaplains gave absolution.

Geoffrey, Bishop of Coutances,
Heard many penitents,
Received their confessions
And blessed them.
He of Bayeuxc did likewise,
Behaving most nobly.
He was the Bishop of the Bessin,
Odo, son of Arlette,
Brother of the Duke on the mother's side.
He supported his brother
With Knights and other men,
Because he was rich in silver and gold.

Rou, verses 7349 to 7360

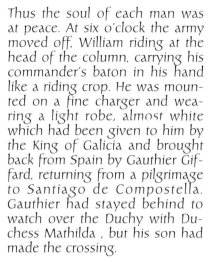

Thus the soul of each man was at peace. At six o'clock the army moved off, William riding at the head of the column, carrying his commander's baton in his hand like a riding crop. He was mounted on a fine charger and wearing a light robe, almost white which had been given to him by the King of Galicia and brought back from Spain by Gauthier Giffard, returning from a pilgrimage to Santiago de Compostella. Gauthier had stayed behind to watch over the Duchy with Duchess Mathilda , but his son had made the crossing.

(Photos G.B.)

(Assor.)

Right beside the Duke fluttered the Papal banner. Traditionally the honour of being the standard bearer should fallen to the Lord of Tosny, but Raoul on that occasion preferred to serve his Duke as a combatant. Gauthier Giffard junior for his part turned down the job which then devolved on Toutain le Blanc of Bec, the son of the Rou the chronicler.

Toutain Rou le Blanc was his name
And his house was at Bec in Caux.
He took it of his own free will
And saluted it humbly,
Carrying it well.

Rou verses 7635 to 7640

A horseman rode up to William. Taillefer was a minstrel at his court who was equally as capable with a sword as at writing poems and singing psalms.

Taillefer, who sang very well,
Rode up to the Duke

And began to sin,
Of the Emperor Charlemagne and Roland,
And Oliver and their vassals
Who died at Roncevaux.
When they had ridden awhile
And the English came in sight,
"Sire", said Taillefer, "thank you.
I have served you for a long time.
There is a service which you owe to me,
And today you shall repay it.
Grant me that I may fall
On the vanguard of battle."
I grant you that" replied the Dike

Rou, verses 8013 – 8029

The vanguard of battle! A tradition of chivalry which reached its peak in the 12th and 13th centuries and a suicide mission what had its origins in the chansons de geste (heroic poems). The Song of Roland, written down at the beginning of the 12th century by the Norman, Turold, introduced a scene concerning Aelroth, nephew of the King of the Moors.

Marcile's nephew rode up on a mule which he managed with a stick, and smiling, said to his uncle, *"dear sire and king, I have served you for so long and have so many sorrows and pains; I have fought and won so many battles. As recompense, grant me the first crack at Roland."* Even though the story of Taillefer is not shown in the Tapestry, it still has many similarities with the

chanson de geste, even a reference to a certain bearded dwarf named as Turold who guarded the horses of William's emissaries to Guy of Ponthieu. Was this the same Turold who wrote the Song of Roland? Certainly the chronology fits this hypothesis. And in that case the epic poem could well have been inspired by events of the Battle of Hastings.

Vital, a knight from Fecamp Abbey, set out to reconnoitre with an escort by way of the copse which screened the English army's movements from view. Proceeding from Blackhorse Hill to the summit of Telham Hill, some hundred metres in height, he saw on the other side of the valley at about the same height as himself, the impressive Saxon battle array, sparking in the first rays of the rising sun which on that day lifted above the horizon at 06.15 Leaving the rear base at Caldbec Hill he advanced to Senlac Hill which was given that name after the battle by the Normans. Vital turned round and set off at the gallop to report to Duke William who realised that he was not going to be able to take Harold by surprise. Thus at seven o'clock he ordered the army to halt and prepare themselves for battle.

The Duke proceeded to put on his hauberk, but it was presented to him back to front. A bad omen?

(G.B.)

Around him a superstitious rumour spread like wildfire as men made the sign of the cross and muttered prayers.

When he decided to arm himself,
He asked for his good hauberk.
A men knelt before the Duke,
Then got up and brought it,
But it was back to front,
A gesture which he did not appreciate.
The Duke's hear passed though
But the coat was in a tangle,
As the front was at the back.
He refused at and sent it back
And those who noticed it,
Became frightened of that hauberk.
"But man", said the Duke, "if I had seen
All that has already happened,
I would refuse to arm myself
And join the battle.
But I have never believed in curses
And never will : I believe in God,
Who acts according to His will.
Only what He wills happens.
I do not like sorcerers,
And I don't believe the fortune-tellers.
It is God alone who commands me.
And my hauberk shall be turned around.
I can give you the clue to this.
It signifies change
In the things that are in progress
And the Prince if the Duchy
Will be a Duke changed into a King!
The Duke who has been will be changed into a King".
And without further thought
He took the hauberk, made the sign of the cross,
Lowered his head and slipped it on,
Laced-up his helmet and belted on the sword
Which a valet brought to him.

Rou, verses 7499 to 7534

As well as St Peter's tooth, William wore a skin pouch around his neck which held some of the relics upon Which Harold had sworn his oath, the ultimate weapon against the latter's perjury. He could easily recognise Harold as could several hundred of the Normans who accompanied him. That us worth mentioning : on the field of batt-

(G.B.)

*Vital, according to the Bayeux Tapestry. (left, by kind permission of the City of Bayeux, **and above,** as per Mogère. (Assor BD))*

le, regardless of who was or was nut under the various banners, he would easily recognise the usurper.

Just when William received Vital's report, Harold was informed of the Norman positions who were less than 200 metres from the Saxons. Their respective hillocks were separated by a depression that formed a small valley.

The two armies were then in view of each other, and on each side the tension was high as it always was when two belligerents realised that battle was about to be joined. Some trembled, even the most battle hardened : the sweat ran down under the helmets and hauberks. In spite of their bravery and determination, many legs were weak, at the sight of the magnitude of the forces confronting them.

Seeing how worried his men were, William ordered the trumpets to be sounded, gathered his officers around him and spoke words of reassurance to them, ordering them to repeat what he said to the other knights and infantrymen. He exhorted them to fight like men with wisdom because they had right and the Good Lord on their side, and added more prosaically that they didn't have a choise : they had to win or die and that there was no question of retreat for the Normans!

The Duke took up position on a patch of land
Where he could see his man as well as
The Barons who surrounded him.
He spoke to them in a loud voice :
"I love you all," he said,
"And I place all my trust in you
I must and I want to thank you
For having crossed the sea for me :
For my honour and my pride.
You have placed your feet on this land.
Whatever it may cost me, I cannot

But reward you accordingly :
I will reward you when I am able
And you will have what is your due.
If I conquer, you conquer
If I take land you will share in it.
But I emphasise
That I didn't come here only
To take what is mine by right,
But to avenge the crimes,
The lies and broken oaths,
Which the men of this country have committed against others :
They have committed treason
But will never do so again".

Rou, verses 7387 – 7414

William's speech produced the desired effect on the noblemen and in response they refused to lose their courage on the threshold of battle.

And they started to cry out,
"Nobody here will be a coward,
None of us is afraid of death
In your cause if need be".
He replied to the saying, "I thank you!
In the name of God don't be afraid
And hit them hard right from the start.
Don't try to take loot :
That will be held in common
And each will receive his share.
None of you can escape
And don't try to run away to save yourselves.
The English have never liked us
Nor have they spared the Normans.
Criminals they were and criminals they are.
They were always false and always will be.
They won't show you any mercy :
Not to the cowards who run away
Nor to the brave, nor to the strong.
Don't get captured by the English
As that will not save you.

If you run back to the sea
But you won't get any further.
You will find neither a boat nor a bridge
Because the sailors and boats have left.
The English will catch up with you
And cut you down without honour.
You would be better off to die fighting
Than fleeing
As you won't save yourselves.
But fight and you will win.
I do not doubt our victory.

We came here for glory
And victory is in our hands.
You can be certain of that".

Rou, verses 7451 to 7488

The nobles shouted in unison, "Dex aie". Reassured about the morale of his army, the Duke occupied himself with studying the terrain in order to plan his strategy. After leading Caldbec Hill the road from Hastings to London passed through a narrow strip of land before widening out into the shape of a hammer on a crest

(G.B.)

ET·VENERVNT

Some 800 metres wide. From there it dropped down to height of 65 metres towards the depression bordered to the east and west by the courses of two streams : between them extended a swampy area which was crossed be the road which climbed again up Telham Hill in the direction of Hastings. For the Normans who were moving up there the road was completely blocked by Harold's troops who were in position along the southern slope of Senlac Hill. There there were traces of cultivated plots, all towards the east. Below, the declivity deepened and thick scrubland guarded against flank attacks while to the west the stream provided a natural barrier. The position was strengthened by a wide hillock some five metres high, which today is covered by trees, but as it was then, still scattered with water-filled holes.

On both sides of the road the slope of Senlac is extremely steep and bordered by ravines. Occupying such a position the Saxons had no chance of retreat other than the way they had come : by way of the throat which formed the handle of the "hammer" of Senlac, through which the local levies were still pouring to reach the battlefield.

The position presented William with certain problems. Even though he had not believed in an attack from the flanks, he realised

that his cavalry would be restricted by the swampy ground between the two streams in the valley. Thus his only option was a direct frontal assault as the Saxons occupied the ridge along its entire length of some 800 metres.

Surrounded by the men of London, Harold planted his personal standard "The Warrior" which featured the figure of a warrior embroidered in fine gold thread, at the highest point on Senlac Hill. His standard bearer carried the banner of Wessex, a sort of windsock on which was a dragon seemingly gnawing at the pole.

His men were quickly organised
And his banner was flown
Carried by his standard bearer

Just at the spot where the Abbey
Commemorating would be built.
"If anyone wants to look for me here,
They will be able to find me".

Rou, verses 6961 – 6968

Just as the Italian Normans were protected by Muslim troops and the Swiss Guard watched over the safety of the Popes, Harold surrounded himself with a foreign bodyguard, his house-carls. Those elite fighting men of Danish origin were descended from the Scandinavian colonisation of eastern England. Proud and courageous Ready for any test, they were ready to die to a man for their master. They wielded with efficiency the long-handled Danish battleaxe as their main weapon supplemented by the sword

hung on their belts. They were protected by chain mail hauberks and conical helmets with nose guards which covered their long hair. They made little use of their shields which they hung over their left shoulders rather than holding them in their hands like the rest of the infantry. They were the best in the entire Saxon army.

To both sides of his field of vision, Harold's men aligned themselves along the crest of Senlac Hill where his Brothers, Gyrth and Leowine, were positioned with their respective contingents, one to the east and the other to the west. They were in the front line together with the Kentish warriors, all of them noblemen.

Behind them the less important thegns (nobles) reinforced the font back up by the peasant levies, essentially gathered in from Kent and Sussex.

That assembly comprised a dozen ranks, more tightly packed at the front than the rear, to make up a compact force of some 8,000 men, all on foot. Harold's position enabled him to see outwards over the heads of his men.

His horses played no part in the battle : they were left in the rear on Caldbec Hill, guarded by local peasantry aided no doubt by children. The absence of cavalry was not the last of the paradoxes apparent in Harold's army. The latter, having taken part in Williams campaign in Brittany would certainly have become aware of the efficacity of the Norman cavalry arm and one wonders why he did not learn from the experience? Nevertheless an army cannot be transformed in a few months and one cannot improvise cavalry fighters which would involve extensive training as well as an equestrian tradition which the Saxons did not have. They always had fought on foot and continued to do so : horses were purely a mans of locomotion for them. However, Harold's army had its own organisation and specialities; Strategy was simple : it consisted of bombarding an enemy with various projectiles and then confronting him in densely packed ranks.

William's troops descended from Telham Hill towards the depression bordered by the two streams. The marshy nature of the terrain forced them to follow the road in column to the bottom of the hill before deploying into line on either side of the road once across the marsh. They advanced onto the slope of Senlac almost within range of the Saxon archers some 200 metres distant. It was by then **0800 hrs.**

The left wing comprised the Breton contingent, the most numerous after the Normans, and they were joined by volunteers from Maine, Anjou and Poitou, all under the command by Alain Fergant, the son of Eudes of Penthièvre. Facing them was the eight metre high hillock which they had to get around to get to grips with the Enemy. The Normans were in the centre, commanded by Duke William assisted by Robert de Mortain and Bishop Odo of Bayeux, surrounded by the Ducal household. A number of Sicilian adventurers had returned to their native Normandy to take part in the expedition, in the hope of gaining new lands.

The right wing was the weakest component in terms of numbers. It was made up of Frenchmen, Flemings and men from Picardy, under the command of Count Eustache of Boulogne and Roger de Beaumont. Roger de Montgomery and William Fitz-Osberne, William's seneschal, were detached with Norman cavalry squadrons as reinforcements. Robert, Roger de Beaumont's was taking part in his first set-piece battle.

Thus the Ducal army comprised three distinct and independent divisions separated on the terrain by corridors which permitted certain movements and designed to permit rapid sorties by the cavalry. Montgomery and Fitz-Osbern had been ordered to fight together depending upon circumstances : one could protect the other if required with the latitude of relative mobility between the French and the Norman divisions.

William on his charger
Ordered Roger de Montgomery
To come before him.

Without hesitation the Duke said to him,
"This is the side you will attack on,
And William, my seneschal,
The son of Osbern, a good vassal
Will follow you
And will attack them with you.

Rou, verses 7645 to 7654

That was what William entrusted to them. Outside his own family, they were the twin pillars of the army and of Normandy. William de Crépon, an intimate friend and Roger de Bellème who held the whole of the south of his Duchy.

Each of the three division was separated into three components. In front there were 1,000 archers, crossbowmen and skirmishers almost entirely without body protection. Behind them were about 3,500 infantry armed with spears, swords and protected by jerkins, shields and helmets. In the third line were the aristocracy, 2,500 knights divided up into squadrons. In reserve to the rear were spare horses guarded by valets.

The presence of crossbowmen at Hastings may seem surprising because that arm had seemed to disappear in the West together with the Roman Empire and not to reappear until the First Crusade. Evidence though can be leaned from texts of the period which emphasised the inadequacy of shields against penetration by crossbow quarrels(bolts) which were fired from their ramps like short missiles when the tensioning device was released.

Those early crossbows were primitive, made entirely of wood with a string that had to be tensioned by hand while the archer used his feet to support the bow against the ground. Nevertheless, their effect was similar to that of a rifle.

Williams aim was to weaken the Saxon front line with his archers, to throw the infantry into any breech thus opened and then project his cavalry at the enemy lines to rout them. Behind the

troops were placed the clergy, the servants and water carriers as well as those too young to fight in the line.

It was thus time for a final attempt at conciliation, made without any real conviction but because it was customary and posterity demanded that everything be seen to be done to avoid a bloodbath between Christians. William advanced with is escort and the Papal banner, up the slope towards the Saxons and asked for a Parley. Harold declined to get involved and sent his brother Gyrth to represent him. William offered an agreement based on respect for the oath sworn at Bayeux and a partition of England : the Dike contenting

The terrain : very broken, the lower parts being below the 60 metre contour whereas the higher parts in the foreground and background rose to some 90 metres, thus there was roughly 50 metres in difference from the lowest to the highest points. ❶ Telham Hill, over 90 metres high and it was from there that William observed the battlefield. His army had marched up from Hastings along the road seen in the foreground with the intention of continuing ❷ by crossing Caldbec Hill (90 metres plus high)on the road to London. At the fork another road ❸ also headed northwards. Between the two summits, however, the terrain dipped down into a narrow declivity ❹, confined by valleys to the east ❺ to the right and west ❻ to the left where the Asten stream spread out to form an area of marsh. Dominating this dip was the Senlac Hill ❼ which also controlled the while countryside and the road to London.

The model which we made exaggerates the relief in comparison with reality. It encloses in real terms an area more than two kilometres wide from east to west and a little less that two kilometres in depth. Nevertheless in reality the terrain is very broken and the Senlac position was an ideal one for Harold's troops. Bounded as it was to east and west by wooded areas, which hindered William from working around the flanks.

(Model and conception, Erik Groult and Georges Bernage/Heimdal)

himself with the earldoms to the south of the Humber.

This was categorically refused and each returned to his lines. Battle was about to be joined.

Into a doubtful outcome

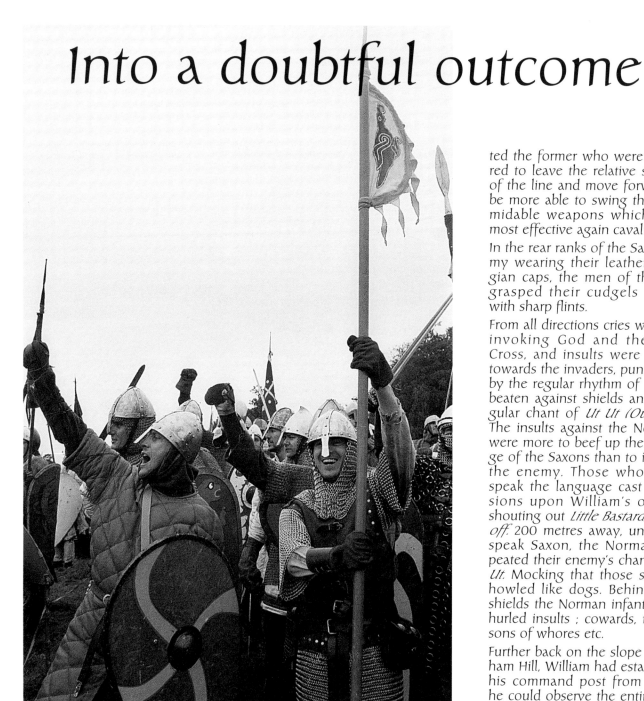

Spread out along the crest of the ridge, the Saxon infantry was hardly visible behind the wall of shields : round Scandinavian ones and kite-shaped Norman patterns – their wearers gave the impression that they were rooted into the ground. Standing firmly they waited to be attacked, firmly grasping their spears or swords. The first line was held by thegns backed by the humbler levies of the fyrd ready to swing their giant axes. Anyone who managed to penetrate the shield wall risked being cut in two by those men, dressed like Vikings with their bushy bears and the flowing locks poking out underneath their helmets, their torsos protected by a leather doublet so strong resistant that it was the equivalent of a mail coat. Using an axe, however, made wearing of a shied impossible and they were carried slug over the left shoulder, rendering the soldier vulnerable to spear thrusts and sword cuts. Axemen were also in the front line alternating with those armed with spears and swords who protec-

ted the former who were prepared to leave the relative security of the line and move forward to be more able to swing their formidable weapons which were most effective again cavalry.

In the rear ranks of the Saxon army wearing their leather Phrygian caps, the men of the fyrd grasped their cudgels tipped with sharp flints.

From all directions cries went up, invoking God and the Holy Cross, and insults were hurled towards the invaders, punctuated by the regular rhythm of swords beaten against shields and a regular chant of *Ut Ut (Out Out)*. The insults against the Normans were more to beef up the courage of the Saxons than to impress the enemy. Those who could speak the language cast aspersions upon William's origins, shouting out *Little Bastard shove off.* 200 metres away, unable to speak Saxon, the Normans repeated their enemy's chant of *Ut Ut.* Mocking that those savages howled like dogs. Behind their shields the Norman infantry also hurled insults ; cowards, traitors, sons of whores etc.

Further back on the slope of Telham Hill, William had established his command post from where he could observe the entire battlefield. He sent signals to his troops to move into line along a similar front to the Saxons, circa 800 metres.

Taillefer galloped among the infantry, towering over them on account of his mount. He left their ranks and amid a bust of acclamations, trotted in front of them, brandishing his sword in the air that sparkled in the morning sunlight. Up on Telham Hill, William and his suite observed the scene and crossed themselves. When the minstrel had trotted the entire length of the front, he sheathed his sword, grabbed a lance and spurred his horse towards Senlac Hill. As he

rounded the minstrel's horse, hacking away at it until its skull was shattered by a sword blow The Norman unsheathed his sword, killed another Saxon and then fell himself, butchered by the enemies' blades.

Taillefer rode straight ahead
And in front of all the others
Struck an Englishman he met
Through his belly and down to the feet
He pierced him with his lance,
Stretching him dead on the ground.
And he killed another one with his sword
And then shouted "come on, come on.
What are you doing? Strike, strike".
The English then surrounded him
And cut him down.

Rou, verses 8030 to 8040

distanced himself from the Norman lines their shouts faded from his hearing to be replaced by the *Ut Ut* if the Saxons, a group of whom had broken away from the shield wall and advanced to meet him.

Taillefer galloped towards them, shouted out *Dex aie* and struck the first blow of the battle. Transfixed, a Saxon fell mortally wounded. His companions sur-

Harold's army was drawn up on the crest of Senlac ❶ where his troops stood shoulder to shoulder : there were more than 7,000 of them. Duke William's army had arrived along the road from Hastings ❷, and had advanced still in column over the hillock at the base of Senlac. The Breton contingent ❸ commanded by Alain Fergeant was placed on the left wing with roughly 400 archers in front of 1000 infantry and 500 knights to the rear. The Norman contingent ❹ took up the centre under the orders of William. The circa 800 archers are represented by the figurines (a) and behind then came the Norman infantry (b), numbering more than 2000 men and then a thousand mounted knights (c). On the right wing were the contingents of William Fitz Osbern and Eustace of Boulogne ❺. There were circa 300 archers in front of 800 infantry, backed up by 400 knights. These figures are taken from Hastings 1066, by Christopher Gravett, published by Osprey. Gravett based them on his estimation of 7,500 men in William's army, and the numbers given for the various contingents are also supposition but are reasonably accurate. (Erik Groult/Heimdal).

For a few moments that seemed to last for an eternity, a funereal silence cloaked the slopes of the two hillocks. Stupefied the two opposing armies contemplated their first casualties. But then the valley between them echoed again to the sounds of war, trumpets insults, howls of rage, swords beating on shields, the whinnying of horses and the hiss of arrows in flight.

The archers had gone into action. They advanced in two regularly spaced ranks, halted at a distance of 50 metres from the Saxons and opened fire. Shooting away from their short bows held in the front of the face, the arrows arced up into the sky and fell like rain on the English lines where the shields were repositioned so as to overlap like tiles on an endless roof covering the

The battlefield seen from the south-west. In the foreground the Asten stream can be seen and the marshy area on the low ground to the west ❶. We see again, from this angle, the Saxon positions ❷, the Bretons ❸, the Normans ❹ and the Franco-Flemings ❺. The allied contingents, all under the orders of Duke William were half way up the slope and still had to cover 200 metres to get to grips with the Saxon front line after the archers had fired off their arrows. It was then 0800 hrs on Saturday 14 October 1066. (Erik Groult/Heimdal)

(Eurouniform)

(Assor)

entire front on Senlac. Some missed their target and caused casualties among the fyrd levies who were still arriving. Volley after volley was launched until the quivers were empty.

On the other side the riposte was weak as there were few archers in the Saxon army. In England the bow was used only for hunting. Naturally there were no crossbows. In addition the battles of Fulford and Stamford Bridge had resulted in the death of many archers. Lacking horses the Wessex men were not able to achieve much at that moment. The lack of Saxon arrows paradoxically proved a handicap for the Normans who could not recover any arrows on the battlefield (some arrows could be fired as many as ten times from one camp to another), and had to retreat to the rear to reequip, thus breaking the rhythm of the attack. Another problem was that the steepness of the slope considerably reduced the penetrating power of the arrows. The crossbow bolts were also ineffective and thus that initial phase had

little impact on the Saxon ranks. The archers retired under a hail of enemy stones, their attack having proved to be without impact.

Then the infantry advanced. Thousands of Bretons, Normans and French moved steadily forward in step under a hail of stones and insults from the Saxons. Some of the attackers carried short-handled axes and maces. Some of them were killed or wounded by the odd arrow or the mass of projectiles, but they regrouped and continued their advance.

You should have heard the cries
On both sides of the conflict.
The Normans knew how to attack
And the English held firm.
They beat at each other ceaselessly.
They were so tough that there was no doubt.
You should have seen that scrap
Of which the memory is famed.

Rou. Verses 8041-8048

The Bretons fought like the Celts with great bravery but without

(Eurouniform)

discipline. They sought individual combat thrusting out ahead and were exhausted when they got up onto the ridge, although it was less steep there than in the south west in front of the French contingent. They threw their spears and fought wildly without any regard for their flanks, with the result that the enemy shields began to box them in as if they were caught in a vice. When the Bretons realised the danger, they managed to escape by making use of their swords, pursued by the furious Saxons as well as a hail of stones.

Half way down the slope the fighting dissolved into isolated scraps often man against man wile the other divisions advanced to contact.

The shock was enormous and the Saxon lines wavered but did not break under the pressure of the disciplines Normans trying to break through the shield wall. It was said that the Saxon infantry were so tightly packed that dead did not even have room to fall and even the wounded were unable to fall back and dies of suffocation. Harold's men were quite content to let the Normans exhaust themselves in such futile and costly assaults. After several minutes of indecisive combat, William sent in part of this cavalry to the rescue.

The cavalry, the speciality of the ducal army was based on the expertise of several centuries and developed in the Christian West, especially in Normandy. What did the warhorses of the 11th century look like? They are shown on the Tapestry as broad-chested mounts, docile under their riders' saddles, eager to charge and as brave as their masters. Neither too large nor particularly frisky, the Norman horses were obviously the result of selective breeding with a view to enhancing their suitability for war. Today, most of the well known equine strains have Arab blood in their veins and in the 11th century that Norman breeds already had this. In 732, the defeat of the Moors at Poitiers led to the capture of numerous horsemen and their mounts. Thus

the blood of the Rotrous of the Perche was improved by the new strains from the East and Mortagne, known as the Moors' town became the cradle of the percheron breed. The First Crusade also occasioned cross-breeding with Arab stallions and the chargers of the Ducal army were more advanced than their contemporaries, an example being William's magnificent mount which had obvious Arab ancestry. The Norman saddle

was quite hard and deep, carved from beech wood with prominent pommel and backrest to hold the rider firmly in position and to save him being unhorsed as a result of the inevitable frontal shocks during a charge. Painted and decorated but without a saddle cloth it was attached by a leather girth just as is the method today and stopped from sliding backwards by a breast strap.

Harness consisted of the usual outfit in leather : bit, bridle and reins but without the strap passing under the throat as was normal with Greek horses. This strap had neither been forgotten nor was unknown to the Normans because one can be seen on panel 16 of the celebrated Tapestry.

The horses could have a simple halter and be managed by means of a collar in the style of the Numidians in the 4th century BC, as in panel 2 although these were Saxon horses. One cannot imagine such a primitive harness system in the Ducal ranks and there is not another example at Hastings in the rest of the Tapestry.

The bit was extremely severe : short at the top and extremely long at the bottom, a powerful lever arm which was applied by the slightest touch on the reins. William's cavalry was certainly very effective but was miles aprt from the precepts of Guérinière, the riding-master of Louis XV, who recommended gentleness and patience to his illustrious

pupil. It is true that the aids available to the rider were limited. He held the reins in his left hand with the lower arm inserted into the straps that held the shield, while the right hand held the sword or lance. The weight of the hauberk too away what little comfort the rider had left : he had to manage the reins, assisted by shouted commands and his body weight, his shoes rested in the stirrups which hung from long leathers. The brass or bron-

Spurred up the slope the horses charged to capture the crest. With their flanks streaming blood they were confused by the Saxons' cries and chants, and the projectiles that glanced off them or hit them about their noses or eyes. Their pathetic whinnying mingled with the agonised cries of the men wounded in that bloody clash of arms.

In order to use their lances, the knights tried to find gaps in the shield wall, at the moment when a Saxon axe was in the air before crashing down on their thighs or their mounts. They did not stay still for long, advancing to get in a blow, turning, retreating and then coming back again. The

ze spurs were as sharp as daggers.

A rider's seat had more to do with the grip exerted by his legs than a natural sense of balance, not that he was deprived of balance, but rather by the constraints imposed by the weight of his equipment. In fact the silhouette of a cavalryman of the 11th century was more akin to that of a cowboy then a modern dressage rider.

What was William's horse really like? The Tapestry shows him variously mounted : in ceremonial dress and unarmed on a chestnut meeting Guy de Ponthieu, but this was a parade horse rather then a *destrier* or charger. Thus called because the owner's squire held it with his right hand when it was not mounted. Later, William was at Dinan on a reddish coloured horse with a blond mane, a chest-strap decorated with besants, carrying a lance with a banner attached and a fleur de lys on his shield : at Bayeux he was similarly mounted which was logical as he was just back from Brittany. Finally at Hastings he was successively mounted on a chestnut, a reddish-brown one and a light grey, probably to show that he had several horses killed under him during the course of the battle.

ensure the front line stayed tightly locked together.

The Normans' shields shattered under the blades and their horses fell. Blood spurted and the wounded screamed their last supplications to God and the saints.

Robert de Beaumont, the father of Robert junior, was in the front line of that charge. Roger de Montgomery managed to break free and distinguished himself fighting against the house carls, piercing them with his lance and avoiding their blood stained axes. As they fell back it was William Fitz Osbern who advanced. The two of them, supported by their squadrons, caused great carnage.

William Malet's shield was split by a sword stroke : the blow was so strong that it went through the shield and embedded itself in the horse's neck which fell down dead under him. That could have cost him his life but the Lord of Montfort came to his rescue aided by William de Vieux-Pont. Combining their efforts they got him into the saddle of another charger which his squire had brought forward.

Neil de Saint-Sauveur did not struggle any less. Using the chest of his horse, that proud baron from the Cotentin bowled over as many Saxons as he could, knocking them off balance and slitting their throats as he passed them with his sword blade.

A Norman knight who had got out in front, but off the hand of a house carl just as he himself

jaws of their chargers suffered under the violent tugs at the bits causing their mouths to bleed. Knights collapsed on top of their horses which had been struck down by blows from the axes of the enemy

The Saxons had spread caltraps over the ground, from which sprouted sharp spikes that pierced the horses' hooves. They stumbled, cried out in pain and turned back with bloody feet, put out of action.

In spite of the violent of the engagement, the English held their positions. Between two cavalry charges the infantry threw their javelins which turned the enemy shields into huge porcupines. The axemen were everywhere, out in front to hack at horses and riders and further back to

The accuracy of this re-enactment on the actual historic battlefield allows a glimpse of just how difficult and exhausting were the Norman attacks on the Saxon position, weighed down as they were by their heavy equipment. They well deserved their victory against Harold's skilfully chosen position .
(photo G.B.)

was about to strike a blow. Another was slashed across the forehead so that blood ran down into his eyes, and beside him, an axeman received the tip of a lance in the back. There was not a single Norman who did not give of his best and there was not a Saxon who did not do his duty.

A vasall of Grenthemesnil
Found himself in great peril that day,
When his horse bolted.
He was lucky not to be thrown
As he was swept along.
His rein had broken
And the horse ran ahead
Galloping towards the English
Who saw him and raised their axes.
But a jab of the spurs
Turned the horse back down into the valley.

Rou verses 8436 – 8448

It was the left wing that suffered the heaviest casualties. Infantry and Breton cavalry retreated in disarray. Abandoning their dead they fled back down the hill. Seeing the disorder on the western side the centre began to retreat as well, not wishing to be left isolated out in front.

As the morning drew to a close and at that stage of the battle the Normans could only entrust their souls to God.

The Bayeux Tapestry (below) shows us how the position selected by Harold was a sort of promontory dominating the battlefield, against which the repeated Norman assaults came to nothing. But once again, it was the Norman cavalry that won the day.

The Duke is Dead!

It was at that stage that William decided to intervene to save the situation. Towards **midday**, flanked by his standard bearer and Odo of Bayeux, he left his station on Telham Hill. Sword in hand he threw himself into the battle in order to regain control of his army. At the head of the Normans and closing with the house carls, William and his horse fell, weighed down by the weight of his hauberk. His charger, the beautiful Spanish stallion, had been killed by a javelin thrust to the chest. A terrible cry went up : *"The Duke is dead".*

The ghastly rumour spread like wildfire through the ducal army. The Duke is dead. The Normans have lost their commander. The Duke is dead. The battle is lost.

The situation was desperate. The Breton knights who were formed up on the patch of ground known ever sinceas the Hillock, withdrew southwards as fast as their tired horses could carry them, going as far as the Asten stream which they plunged into. Knights and infantry became en-

Having fired their arrows to little result, the archers ❶ withdrew to the rear on reserve with the baggage and servants. The infantry attack on the Saxon lines was a heavy one, but on the Breton wing they were unable to gain a foothold and retreated in disorder ❷, pursued by part of the Saxon right wing ❸ who left their positions. The panic also spread among the ranks of the Normans ❹, who believed that Duke William had been killed. Part of the Breton contingent had been hemmed into the swampy area ❺. The situation for the invaders was precarious.

tangled and slipped on the marshy banks of the stream encumbered by their equipment where they were caught and massacred by their pursuers.

William managed to pick himself up. The English threw themselves on him but he managed top hold then at bay with his sword and he even managed to knock some over by using his shield as a ram. His intention was to obtain another mount and he waved his bloody sword to cut off the retreat of a knight fleeing in panic, who refused to stop. But, as he swept by, William seized his foot and unhorsed the coward. He mounted the horse and galloped off having recovered his helmet so that everyone would recognise him. Sensing disaster, Eustace of Boulogne had seized the papal banner from the hand of Toutain

The Duke is Dead!

de Bec who was obviously overwhelmed by events. The banner fluttered proudly in the breeze and the army took heart again. "No, he isn't dead – he's fine and will lead us to victory". William cried out : "take a good look at me. I am alive and with God's help we are going to win

But Odo and then William managed to rally those fleeing and mounted a counter-attack with the Norman cavalry. The Saxons who had advanced were surrounded and cut to pieces on the Hillock ❶ where Harold's two brothers were among the victims. The Normans had managed to re-establish the situation but the Saxon right wing had lost its front ranks which had set off in pursuit of the Bretons ❷. The Normans and Franco-Flemings returned to Senlac and started a fresh attack ❸ (Erik Groult/Heimdal

this battle. Don't run away. Flight will only bring you dishonour and death because none of you will escape the English unless you defeat them".

Taking his cue from William, Odo brandished his mace and addressed the cowards.

They wanted to abandon everything,
not knowing where to escape to.
When Odo the brave cleric
Who is dedicated to Bayeux,
spurred them on and said
"Stop, Don't move, keep calm.
Don't be afraid of anything, because
God wants us to be victorious".

Rou verses 8105 – 8112

William recovered his sword and rode up and down on the battle-field, rallying the men trying to flee and collected them back on Telham Hill. There he reasoned with them and reassured, they reformed their units and returned to the slopes of Senlac.

There remained the problem on the left wing. In the marsh with their backs to the stream, the Bretons were about to be submerged by several hundred Saxons who had left their defensive positions to take part in the slaughter, hoping for a rapid conclusion. Harold yielded to his impulsive nature and gave the order to counter-attack.

But suddenly the pursuers found themselves surrounded by William and his knights who fell upon the hapless Saxons with sword and lance just as if it was a training exercise. A few managed to escape up onto the Hillock where they prepared to defend themselves as if in a fort. Dozens of knights threw themselves into the assault but some

of them stumbled into the water-filled holes and others slipped. The rest of them, however, cleared the position leaving only the bodies of the slain behind.

All of a sudden the Bretons recovered themselves, evacuated the wounded and joined in the slaughter until not a single Englishman was left alive to call for mercy. The Hillock was a scene of frightful carnage. In a matter of minutes under the horrified eyes of Harold and his men, all those who had believed in a swift victory, house carls, thegns and fyrd levies, had rendered their souls to God.

That first assault caused heavy casualties on both sides and among the Saxon victims were Gyrth and Leowine, Harold's two brothers. The Norman chroniclers, generally favourable towards Gyrth, no doubt to contrast him with Harold, pretended that he had been killed by William in person but that was no doubt a chivalric embellishment. It is more likely that the brothers were killed while taking part in the counter-attack at the head of their respective contingents, paying the price for Harold's impetuosity.

The sun broke through the clouds as if to highlight the hundreds of bodies littering the ground. The armies regained their initial positions, profoundly exhausted. The Normans had avoided disaster by a hair's breadth – if Harold had thrown his entire army into the melée he would have undoubtedly won the battle.

Hostilities ceased for a while, not because of some truce negotiated by commanders, but simply suspended because nobody was left capable of fighting. Priests and water-carriers moved among the dying and the wounded who had been carried to the rear, while the rider-less horses that were galloping here and there were caught. It was necessary to

(Assor)

reconstitute the ranks, replenish the archers' quivers, check weapons and re-sharpen swords.

There was also a need to rebalance the various units to make good the losses, so that each one could fight coherently. The Breton adventure had cost Harold dearly who had to redeploy a considerable number of combatants to his right wing which had been seriously weakened during the course of the morning.

William gathered together his staff, Robert de Mortain, Odo de Bayeux, Eusrace de Boulogne, Roger de Beaumont, William Fitz-Osbern, Roger de Montgomery and Alain de Penthievre. All were in agreement that the archery had proved ineffective and the infantry was incapable of breaking into the Saxon lines. The best infantry in the western world could only be defeated by the best cavalry. Servanys and squires busied themselves

around the chargers, dressing their wounds, serving them a ration of oats and bathing them in the streams in the valley.

William had to win the battle by sunset as his army would not survive to see another sunrise because Harold's reinforcements would catch the Normans in a trap. More than ever the alternatives were expressed in three words – conquer or die.

The defeat of a king

(Assor)

The battle got underway again at around 1400 hours. Eustace de Boulogne had returned to the left wing and Toutain de Bec was again carrying the papal banner. Once again the cavalry was unable, however, to break down the human fortress built up on the ridge during the morning and it was impossible to outflank the position owing to the unevenness of the ground as well as the density of the vegetation. William took an active part in the fighting. He was worried about another stampede and took steps to deal immediately with any such event.

flight was only simulated. William had learned his lesson from the sad experience with the Bretons during the morning and had used the pause in the fighting to organise a cunning new tactic.

They were agreed among themselves
That if they would extend the English
And pretend to be trying to flee,
So that the English would pursue them.
By tempting them down into the fields

slaughtered them where they stood aided by the infantry who had opportunely regained their cohesion. Why did Harold's soldiers allow themselves to be thus entrapped? Were they not aware of the disaster that had befallen the pursuers of the Bretons a few hours earlier? Did they believe that this time it would be all right? It always appeared that in the heat of action, they rant simply full tilt towards their destiny. Even worse, the same manoeuvre was repeated during the course of the afternoon, probably in the centre with equal success.

What was remarkable was the extraordinary cohesion of the Norman units concerned, used to working together during the previous months and for some of them for several years under the orders of the same Lords, who had been taken into William's confidence about his idea of a simulated retreat and who, at the right moment, had no difficulty in assembling their men under their banners to carry out the Duke's orders. One can state that it was William who really invented mediaeval cavalry management in the West. He did not have everything his way that 14 October, however, suffering the loss of two more chargers killed under him before the end of the battle. In fact chargers became quite rare because numerous knights had to seek remounts during the course of the engagement.

The two false retreats were a veritable stroke of genius which proved decisive. It was only the imminent setting of the sun which made a swift conclusion necessary.

The Saxons began to give way. The ten closely packed and disciplined ranks along the crest of the hill had been dramatically thinned by the three disastrous sorties. The best of the warriors were recumbent in the grass in pools of blood, and those who replaced them were only fyrd levies, ready for a fight but poorly equipped and armed. It was only Harold's household troops that were holding out, his house carls and some thegns, but for how

He gave an order which quickly spread along his right wing. Several groups of infantry and a few French knights advanced into the attack, throwing their javelins and exchanging sword cuts with the Saxon front line, then withdrew, hurling insults. As they retreated, once again the English pursued them, excited at the prospect of easy booty and attracted by the hauberks and helmets of the French. They were mistaken, however, for the

Where if they could separate them,
The easier it would be to attack them.
Their strength would be weakened
And they would be lore easily discomforted.

Rou verses 8179 – 8188

According to the prepared plan, the knights surrounded the Saxons who had unwisely left the security of their lines, and long? William knew that he had to defeat them, but his own troops were exhausted after the repeated attacks. Lacking mounts, many of the knights were reduced to fighting on foot. In addition, Senlac Hill, which fully deserved it name, was strewn with numerous obstacles : bodies of both horses and men were scattered all over the slope and hindered the advance of the living. William decided to use those sad victims of the vicious slaughter of the battle. He brought forward his archers who were almost intact and had been preserved for just such an eventuality – the next stage of the battle would be in their hands. Half of them were positioned on the slope just as they had been at the outset of the battle. The other half crept up the hill until they were only a few paces from the Saxons, where they hid behind the piles of bodies. Many of the horses were still alive, whinnying in agony and beating the air with their legs; The first group loosed their arrows high into the air, forcing the Saxons to lift their shields to protect themselves against the plunging fire. At the same moment the other archers opened up with their bows level, shooting a hail of metal into the unprotected enemy ranks. Time and time again the action was repeated, sowing panic among

(Assor)

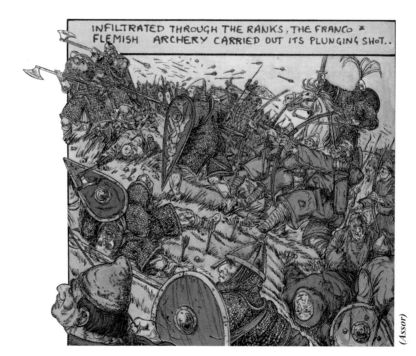

(Assor)

The figurines place on the model of the battlefield give an idea of the terrain and the obstacles confronting the Norman during the later stages of the battle : the archers, further back, brought down plunging fire on the Saxons while the cavalry and infantry broke into their last ranks. Harold was wounded by an arrow while he was still in the middle of his house carls (300 at the start of the battle). The lightly armed fyrdmen were soon destroyed. (Erik Groult/Heimdal)

the Saxons who did not know how to protect themselves against the hail of death raining down on them. They raised and then lowered their shields in an ineffective defence. Dead or wounded the English fell, until the archers ran out of arrows to fire.

Than the cavalry returned to the charge, hurling their javelins, knocking over the wounded and trampling on the dead. They changed weapons to strike the enemy with their lances, swords and maces to finish the job started by the archers. It was time to screw up one's courage and to

(Assor)

create one's own legend in individual combat.

Experiencing his first battle, Robert de Beaumont, conducted himself as a worthy son of his father. He was reliable and dealt with anyone he encountered, to such an extent that the chronicle of William of Poitiers made him out to have been one of the finest combatants of the day.

(Assor)

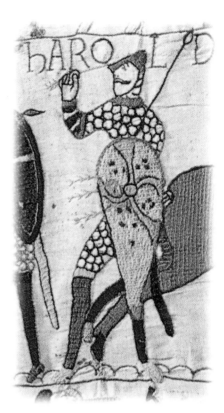

Robert Fitz-Erneis went for the big prize. He fixed his gaze on Harold's personal standard with its gold-embroidered warrior. Spurring his charger forward, he cut down a house carl with his sword, grabbed the pole of the trophy but perished under the giant axes before he could turn to seek safety in the Norman ranks.

The men of Kent and Essex sold their lives dearly and fought like enraged lions during the ultimate stages of the battle. A Danish axe struck William's helmet but before the man wielding it could rejoin his rank he was killed by the lance of one of the Duke's bodyguards.

But then it was time to finish the matter. A group of some twenty

(SB.)

(SB.)

knights had sworn to kill or at least capture the oath-breaker of Bayeux, and William launched them at Harold's position. Four of them reached him, but the king was but a shadow of his former self. One of the arrows from the earlier volleys had fixed itself in his right eye. He had managed to wrench it out with terrible pain and was bleeding copiously.

Thus it was that an arrow arrived,

(G.B.)

King Harold is dead. A few Saxons continue to fight while others flee. ❶ Duke William, his Norman knights and allied troops are in control of the hill they were to call Senlac ❷. Some knights have set off to pursue the fugitives ❸. (Erik Groult – Georges Bernage/Heimdal)

Falling out of the sky.
It struck Harold in the right side
of his face
Taking out his eye.
Harold enraged pulled it out.
He extracted it but it broke.
His head was in such pain
That he had to support it on his
shield.

Rou verses 8161 – 8168

Blind in one eye, Harold could still count of his house carls, ready to fight to the last. Like the four horsemen of the apocalypse, Eustace de Boulogne, Hugh de Montfort, Hugh de Ponthieu, son of Guy and Gauthier Giffard, the young Lord of Longueville threw themselves at the usurper with all the force that their blood drenched spurs could impart to their chargers.

The first one's lance pierced the royal shield and embedded itself in his chest while that of the second opened the king's stomach. The third one's sword cut his throat. At circa **1600 hours,** Harold expired and then Gauthier Giffard taking his sword hacked at the left thigh of the corpse. That inglorious feat of arms led to him being exiled to the east of the Duchy by William.

Harold was dead but his bodyguard fought on until the death of the last royal thegn and house carl. Not one of them managed to escape. The royal banners were captured and the standard of Wessex was trampled underfoot. The one with the golden warrior was brought to William who sent it to Pope Alexander II as a sign of his divine victory and in gratitude for the papal support in the conquest of England. The standard of St. Peter fluttered in its place among a heap of Saxon bodies.

The crest was hemmed in on both flanks by the men who did not have anyone left to fight, and the clearance of Senlac hill began. Odo was ordered to take charge of securing the rear areas where fyrd reinforcements were still tricking in late, guided by the sounds of combat. Once they realised that all was over, they slipped away under cover of darkness as night fell. There was total confusion in the rear areas of the battlefield. The local peasant levies seized any errant horse and took to their heels at the gallop. Others tried to withdraw on foot, leading horses which had been tethered behind the Saxon lines and made their way back through the forest harried by the ducal army. Cavalry and infantry were all mixed together, struck down by lances, arrows and sword cuts. Scores of the wounded died in the forest or alongside the roads.

Bursts of fighting still broke out around Caldbec Hill and the surrounding area, where the English who knew the terrain well, mounted ambushes, killing a good number of Normans, Bretons and French, lured into the forest by their hatred of the fugitives. As the sun sank behind Caldbec Hill near the place known as the Hoar Apple Tree, a ditch hidden by dense vegetation and undergrowth was nut seen by the pursuers and just behind it on a spot of firm ground, a group of house carls waited for the Norman knights. The latter, spying their quarry, galloped towards them with drawn swords, only to tumble into the ditch filled with water and brambles. There they fell and became entangled, dying under the weight of their horses. The ditch became known as the *Malfosse*. The Saxons fell upon

(G.B.)

the knights, massacring them with their swords. Thus, many brave men who had survived the rigours of battle, perished as a result of their own impetuosity

Eustace de Boulogne observed the carnage and realised that it was useless to continue the pursuit, and rode off to find William. The latter's helmet was dented, his horse covered with blood and lumps of flesh were stuck to his skin. All he was holding in his hand was the broken shaft of a lance. Eustace begged him to recall the men and stop the slaughter. The night fell quickly and the moon did not appear before midnight : in a matter of moments the whole countryside was plunged into total darkness. Having been

granted his request, the Count of Boulogne let loos a groan : an arrow had penetrated his coat of mail and had lodged between his shoulders. There was blood trickling from his mouth and his nostrils. He was carried off unconscious and no one doubted for a moment that he would succumb to that terrible wound.

It was all over. The Normans' torches lit up the crest of Senlac Hill. William had set up camp for the night there and declared as an act of grace that he would build a new abbey on the spot – Battle Abbey. There where Harold had died and where the banner of St. Peter was flying, would be built the high altar of the abbey church.

(S.B.)

In this final view of the battlefield model, some Norman knights who had set off in pursuit of fleeing Saxons, came upon a steep depression in which flowed a stream known as Manser's Shaw, where they were attacked by certain of the fugitives and were unhorsed in the valley ❶, *which the Normans named Malfosse on account of the tragic death of certain of their comrades. Some of the fleeing Saxons took the road to London which stood open to the Normans as well* ❷. *There, where King Harold died* ❸, *William the conqueror ordered Battle Abbey to be built.*
(Erik Groult – Georges Bernage/Heimdal).

The Saxons had fought three major battles within three weeks and the last one had been the most violent and sanguinary that the Island had known since the Roman conquest. Tensed ever since the dawn, Williams' nerves relaxed. Still mounted on his exhausted horse, he examined the line of the crest littered with Saxon bodies, in the light of the flickering torches. For the first time that day he saw nothing but human beings while all around him echoed the cries of victory down into the valley and across to Telham Hill. As he listened to the shouts of "Montjoie, St. Michael, Dex Aie", floating up towards him he was overcome with emotion at the sight of all those courageous Saxons, all brave men who had died for their loyalty and who, but for the tide of battle would have become his subjects.

(Assor)

After the battle

Battle Abbey. (G.B.)

On Sunday 15 October 1066, the dawn rose on thousands of mainly naked corpses as the scavengers had already been at work. Others were still at their grisly task fighting over the terribly mutilated bodies with the hordes of carrion eaters cleaning up the battlefield. Hauberks and leather jerkins were fine prizes as was an undamaged sword. A dented helmet could be hammered out and a broken blade recovered. Even the simpler garments, shoes, leggings, belts, were stripped from the mortal remains of those who no longer needed them, and neither was the harness neglected. There was enough left to equip several squadrons!

The first to help themselves were evidently the soldiers at the end of the battle, as well as those engaged in the pursuit. They were followed by the Norman auxiliaries and the horde of non-combatants who also profited from the victory to which they had contributed. By the following morning the macabre clean-up had been more or less accomplished, leaving the bodies that had been overlooked in the thickets far from the scene of combat, located only by the flocks of crows which wheeled overhead. The borders of the Bayeux Tapestry are richly illustrated with scenes of the pillage where one can see hauberks being stripped from the naked bodies,

minus arms, heads and legs. Also to be seen are the scavengers swapping items of booty : a javelin for a shield, a helmet for an axe.

Without exception, only the Saxons were completely stripped and the fighters of the Norman army were entitled to more consideration, their bodies being gathered up and identified where possible. They were given a Christian burial in a minimum of clothing and where possible under their shields as was customary. The rest of their equipment was sent to their families or divided up among their esquires and servants.

How many of the 7,000 combatants in the ducal army died on that tragic day? According to historians, at least 2,000, which does not appear excessive taking into account the number of attacks, assaults and withdrawals during the engagement. The losses on the other side were evidently far heavier if one considers the almost suicidal tactics of the Saxons who chose to die rather then submit to the invaders of their lands, as well as those killed as a result of the simulated retreats and in the final slaughter. : probably between 4 and 5,000 in all. The Normans did not take prisoners and how could one stop those soldiers who had fought from dawn to disk, face to face and for whom each hour that passed provided more dead to avenge.

Elfwig, the Abbott of Winchester, died together with twelve of his monks. Leofric, Abbott of Peterborough, fell mortally wounded, but survived in agony, to be evacuated to die among his community. While the Normans were being buried with the aid of the prayers of the priests that were present, the Saxon families set out to find their loved ones, which was permitted by William. But those nobody claimed had to wait as the Duke had other matters on his mind. He had to involved himself with his own dead and think about his march on London where he would be crowned. To make good his losses he sent emissaries back over the Channel, mainly to Normandy, who took news of the victory.

The bodies of Gyrth and Leowine were found not far from that of their brother, having probably been brought to him after their deaths as they had fallen down towards the valley in the sortie against the fleeing Bretons. They were given Christian burial.

As for Harold, that was a more delicate matter. On the one hand, William reckoned that the oath-breaker who had been excommunicated the previous spring, had no right to the offices of the Church. In addition he believed that the Saxons would regain their national pride and thus Harold would become a hero of the land and a martyr to Norman oppression. On the other hand, how could he be recognised among the pile of naked and mutilated bodies? Senlac was strewn with corpses around the Papal banner, each as disfigured as its neighbour and any one of them could well be the son of Earl Godwin. The mistress of the dead king was the only one person capable of identifying him - the beautiful Edith Swan Neck, so called because of the grace of her deportment and the elegance of her long neck.

She had watched the whole of the battle standing at the foot of an ancient oak on the south-west slope of Caldbec. She was allowed to wander among the bodies and finally identified one of them as her lover, thanks to certain distinguishing marks that even his own mother did not know about.

Gytha, mother of Harold and his two brothers presented herself to William and offered the Duke his own weight in gold for the right to recover the body, but he turned down the offer and refused to part with the body that might well become a relic. William would have preferred to destroy and disperse the remains of his adversary but was finally convinced to allow him to be buried. He entrusted the job to a Norman knight who had distinguished himself on the battlefield and who had known Harold personally. William Malet had lands in the Caux where he was the Lord of Graville, but had lived at the court of Edward the Confessor and had married an Englishwoman. At a place kept secret, he had a Celtic type of stone cairn raised on top of a cliff overlooking the Channel near the original Norman camp and had the following words engraved on it : "O Harold, by order of the Duke, you rest here as a king, always to guard the coast and the sea." The following century Harold's remains were transferred to Holy Cross Abbey at Waltham in Essex, which he had founded.

(City of Bayeux.)

On the site of the Saxon camp on Caldbec Hill where Harold had passed the night before the battle, William gave orders for a triumphal cairn to be raised to celebrate his victory, at the place still called Montjoie. Then he returned to his fortified encampment at Hastings where he waited for the submission of the Saxon nobles, in vain, because not a single one presented himself.

On 20 October he left Hastings for Dover and on the way, burned Romney as he blamed the town for massacring two crews from his invasion fleet. Dover submitted followed by Canterbury, Winchester and Wallingford.

The Earls Edwin and Morcar, victors of the battles of Fulford and Stamford Bridge, who had declined to join Harold in engaging the Normans took refuge in Northumberland, finally submitting to William after his coronation.

That event took place in Westminster Abbey on Christmas Day 1066 after a march of more than 500 kilometres. Archbishop Stigand who had placed Edward the Confessor's crown on Harold's head, was turned down to perform the same rite for William. He chose instead, Ealdred, Archbishop of York, who proceeded to celebrate the ritual, which caused a tumult of approval to break out. Believing that a riot had started, the troops on guard outside the Abbey, started to torch the surrounding houses and cut down any Saxon who ventured to look out of his door. Thus it was in the middle of the surrounding tumult that the Dike of Normandy became the King of England. It was to take him three years to cement his power and pacify the rebellious counties, building in the process several hundred castles, many of which still exist today. It was easy for him to distribute lands among the victors of Hastings as he had promised, as almost all the Saxon high nobility had been killed. Bishop Odo was made Earl of Kent with the task of holding Dover. His other brother, Robert de Mortain, received Cornwall, Devon, Dorset and Somerset, plus lands in Kent and Yorkshire as fiefdoms, making him the greatest landowner after William himself.

He gave Hertfordshire, Norwich, Canterbury and a job as the equivalent of a viceroy, shared with Odo, to his intimate friend, William Fitz-Osbern. The Count of Bellème, Roger de Montgomery reigned in Shropshie where a town on the Welsh border bears his name. In Sussex, he held Chichester and Arundel, where he built one of the most important castes in England.

The whole of Lincolnshire and part of Yorkshire went to Alain de Penthièvre while Hugh d'Avranches received York and Chester. William de Varenne settled on the Humber, in Norfolk and Lewes. Hugh de Grenthemesnil received Winchester and Onfroy de Teilleul, Hastings. Richard Fitz-Gilbert was granted lands in Suffolk and Kent and the Bishop of Coutances, Geoffroy de Montbray on the Avon. Geoffroy de Mandeville was rewarded with lands in Essex, etc.

There is nothing more to be said about the Saxon nobility. Not one warrior who survived Hastings received any grant of land. That was the price of the bloodshed at Senlac on 14 October 1066.

Biographical notes

(Assor)

Adelise : one of the daughters of William of Normandy, promised in marriage to Harold in 1064 in return for his support in ensuring the succession of William after the death of Edward the Confessor.

Alain Fergeant : Count of Penthièvre and commander of the Breton contingent at Hastings.

Aldgyth : Widow of the Welsh king, Gruffyd ap Llyelwn, who married Harold in the spring of 1066.

Alexander II : Pope from 1061 to 1072. Pleased with William's support for the Church, he officially blessed the conquest of England.

Canute : King of England (1016 – 35) and of Denmark (1018 – 35). Son of Sven, King of Denmark and second wife of Emma of Normandy.

Edward the Confessor : King of England (1042 – 66). Son of Emma of Normandy and the Anglo-Saxon king Ethelred. Had himself no children and designated his cousin William of Normandy as his successor.

Edwin : Earl of Mercia.

Emma : Sister of Richard II, fourth Duke of Normandy and William of Normandy's great-aunt. She married Ethelred, King of England in 1002 and later, Canute, King of both England and Denmark   She died on 5 March 1052.

Ethelred II : Anglo-Saxon King (978 – 1016). First husband of Emma of Normandy and father of Edward the Confessor.

Geoffrey de Montbray : Bishop of Coutances. Played a prominent role in the invasion, the battle and the conquest of England.

Godwin. Created Earl of Wessex by Canute. Married Gytha, a Danishwoman, and was the father of Harold Godwinson.

Guillaume (William) Fitz-Osbern : Son of Osbern de Crépon. Became Duke William's tax gatherer and closest friend.

Guillaume (known as the Bastard) : 7th Duke of Normandy 1035 – 87). Born at Falaise in 1027, the son of Robert II (The Magnificent) and Arlette. The Norwegian Viking chieftain, Rollo, William's ancestor, had received Normandy as a fiefdom in 911 from Charles II (The Simple), King of France. William was King of England from 1066 – 1087.

Guy de Bourgogne : Cousin of William of Normandy. Was behind a baronial rebellion in the west of the duchy that was put down in 1947. Underwent a siege in his castle at Brionne which lasted for three years, before being pardoned and having his lands returned.

Gyrth : The youngest brother of Harold. Earl of East Anglia. Presented by the Norman chroniclers as an example of an honest enemy who could be respected. Killed at Hastings.

Harald Hardrada : King of Norway. Son of Sigurd. The last of the great heroes of the Nordic sagas. Made a secret pact with William of Normandy to partition England, but was killed at Stamford Bridge.

Harold Godwinson : Earl of Wessex and son of Godwin. He swore an oath to William to recognise him as King of England but was persuaded to take the crown for himself on the death of Edward the Confessor.

Leowine or Lewine : Earl of Essex and a brother of Harold. Killed at Hastings.

Mathilda (Mahaut in French) : Daughter of Baudouin V, Count of Flanders, married Duke William in 1050.

Malcolm : King of Scotland. Supported Tostig against Harold.

Morcar : replaced Tostig as Earl of Norrthumberland

Odo de Bayeux : Half-brother of William of Normandy, son of Arlette and Herluin de Conteville. He was the instigator of the Bayeux Tapestry.

Robert de Mortain : Half-brother to William and in charge of the organisation of the ducal army.

Roger de Montgomery : One of the most powerful of the Norman aristocrats. William married him to Mabel de Bellème to cement the allegiance of the southern part of the Duchy.

Taillefer : a minstrel who struck the first blow at Hastings, according to the chronicles of Guy d'Amiens, Wace and Benoit de Saint-Maure.

Tostig : Brother of Harold and Earl of Northumberland. Rebelled against his brother and was killed at Stamford Bridge.

Turold : author of the *Song of Roland.* Was perhaps the same Turold featured on the Bayeux Tapestry.

Wace : Norman chronicler, born in Jersey circa 1110, possibly the grandson of Toustein, chamberlain to Duke Robert II. Wace was a clerk at the court of Henry I, youngest son of the Conqueror, later a clerk at Caen and canon of Bayeux. Author of the *Roman de Brut* in 1155 and the *Roman de Rou,* between 1160 and 1174.

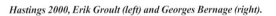

Hastings 2000, Erik Groult (left) and Georges Bernage (right).

Achevé d'imprimer
Sur les presses de l'Imprimerie OCEP
Dépôt légal 1er trimestre 2002